GEORGE PERC

HISTORICAL GUIDE

TO

MALTA AND GOZO

Elibron Classics
www.elibron.com

Elibron Classics series.

© 2005 Adamant Media Corporation.

ISBN 1-4021-7024-6 (paperback)
ISBN 1-4212-8348-4 (hardcover)

This Elibron Classics Replica Edition is an unabridged facsimile
of the edition published in 1872 by P. Bonavia,
Malta.

Elibron and Elibron Classics are trademarks of
Adamant Media Corporation. All rights reserved.

This book is an accurate reproduction of the original. Any marks, names, colophons, imprints, logos or other symbols or identifiers that appear on or in this book, except for those of Adamant Media Corporation and BookSurge, LLC, are used only for historical reference and accuracy and are not meant to designate origin or imply any sponsorship by or license from any third party.

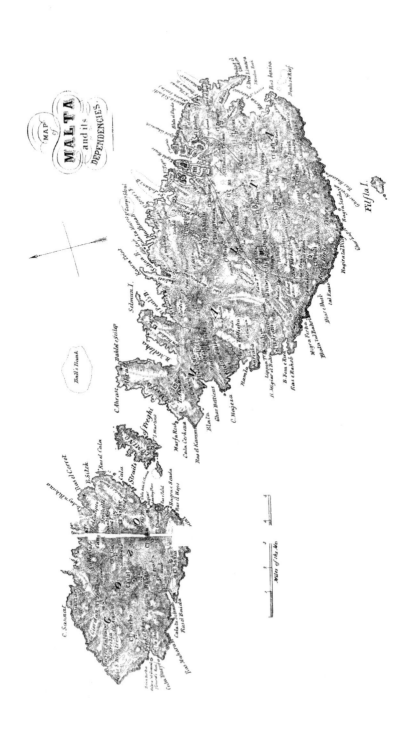

MAP of MALTA and its DEPENDENCIES

Miles of the Sea

HISTORICAL GUIDE

TO

MALTA AND GOZO

BY

G. PERCY BADGER.

FIFTH EDITION.

MALTA

P. BONAVIA,—PRINTER.

MDCCCLXXII.

ADVERTISEMENT.

The fourth Edition of this very interesting and useful work being exhausted, a new and improved one has been compiled containing the latest information as to the trade, commerce, laws, festivals, Public buildings, Churches, and other things and places of interest to gentlemen visiting these Islands.

We have also found it necessary to draw up many fresh statistical tables — correcting errors or noting changes — and suppressing whatever was of little use or interest in former editions.

Our work will be found to contain full and correct information as to the state of these Islands up to the present date. — We therefore hope to enjoy the patronage of gentlemen travellers and of the public in general. — This guide will be of use to students and others, and a most suitable Souvenir to absent friends of a place visited by St. Paul the Great Apostle of the Gentiles.

PREFACE.

FIOR DEL MONDO is the ardent lan—
guage of the love of our country, and
though Malta, which has received the
superlative appellation from its devoted
children, is but a rock, yet " a rock
is a rock" all the world through : while
the glory of the sky which overlooks
Malta, the noble port which indents its
rugged Margin, as also the peculiarity
of its position with regard to neighbouring tracts of the earth, render it altogether a rock singularly interesting, and of
vast intrinsic importance.

The sky, and air, and country of Malta
are African; but its life and civilization
are European. And here, whilst we have
all the fervid glow of a clowdless bound-
less atmosphere,—here, where the orange
grove yields its golden treasures, and the

rosy grape in all its lashious freshness tempts the gazing eye,—we have also, in delightful combination, all the arts, sciences and purities of glorious Europe, which stretches her enlightened sceptre over all lands.

Formerly the bulwark of Christendom against the bloody banner of Islamism and infidelity, and exerting a salutary influence o'er the desolations of Africa, also decisive checks to the infamous piracies of the Barbary coast, Malta, now also, in our own times, exerts a still nobler because a moral influence, upon the shores of the Mediterranean, and occupies under the benign and all powerful flag of Great Britain, a prouder attitude than even during the most renowned days of her chivalrous story, under the sovereignty of the Knights of St. John of Gerusalem.

A writer, then, who attempts some illustration of the past and present history of so remarkable a country as Malta, together with the peculiar features of its social and political state, however humble his efforts, or contradicted his plan, may venture, without the slightest charge of arrogance, to anticipate the good wishes and the support of the public.

The chief design has been, in the following papers, to afford the numerous English travellers who are continually going to and coming from the Levant, now on pleasure, now on business, and in their route making a shorter or longer stay at Malta, some assistance in the knowledge or investigation of these islands. The late facilities offered by steam navigation to all the curious and the learned, to make researches in the Mediterranean seas, have greatly increased the number of Strangers in Malta;—as also, the facilities and conveniences, which the generosity of the truly paternal government of Malta has granted to foreign shipping, have equally augmented the concourse of travellers and strangers in this far famed port.

Here travellers may repose after a long voyage at sea, and even attempt the restoration of their health in case of unlooked for indisposition; and during their hours of quiet and solitude, they may perhaps be agreable occupied with a cursory examination of the things which this brief history points out.

The author has confined himself to objects of utility in general, but has not entirely passed over those of elegance, of science, and of antiquities. And whatever credit he may receive for his labours, he doubts not, that his intentions will be fairly and indulgently construed. At any rate this being the first book in the English language ever attempted, on so limited and portable a scale, in illustration of Malta, he trusts that if he does not entirely succeed in his object, he will have the gratification of having pointed out the way to others, who may follow him in that path which is always noble and philanthropic,—that of making one part of humanity acquainted with another, and of adding to the general stock of the knowledge of the world, by investigating mankind they exist in a geographical situation, political and social state, and and all the peculiarities of mind and feeling.

PART FIRST

HISTORY

OF MALTA.

PART FIRST.

HISTORY OF MALTA.

FROM ITS EARLY SETTLEMENT DOWN TO THE PRESENT TIME.

Preliminary Observations—Settlement of the Phœnicians —Greeks—Carthaginians—Romans — Goths — Emperors of Constantinople—Arabs—Defeat of Emperor's Expedition—Count Roger—Rebellion of the Arabs—Emperors of Germany—King of Aragon and Castile—Charles V. of Germany—Arrival of the Knights of St. John—Their first Acts—Malta besieged by the Turks—Confiscation of several of the Commanderies—Arrival of the French—Siege of Malta—Dreadful state of the town—Appearance of the British Fleet—The French capitulate—Malta ceded to the British Crown.

THE early history of almost every nation is involved in obscurity, and it would be quite foreign to our purpose, to enter into an investigation of the several opinions, which have been advanced by different authors, as to the primitive inhabitants of the island, the origin of its name, its early form and government, and the various natural causes which have operated to reduce it to its present size and shape. We shall content ourselves, by giving the reader a short sketch of what seems to be the most probable, and least fabulous account of the various settlements formed here by different nations, until it fell into the hands of its present possessors.

An ancient author writes, cancerning this island "Malta is furnished with many and very good harbours, and the inhabitants are very rich, for it is full of all sorts of artificers among whom there are excellent weavers of fine linen. Their houses are very stately and beautiful, adorned with graceful eaves and pargetted with white plaster. The inhabitants are a colony of Phœnicians, who, trading as merchants, as far as the western coast, resorted to this place on account of its commodious ports, and convenient situation for maritime commerce; and by the advantages of this place, the inhabitants frequently became famous both for their wealth and their merchandise" (*). From this quotation it appears that the Phœnicians were very early, if not the first settlers of this island; and the learned Bochart considers them the same with the Phœnicians, mentioned by Homer, generally taken for the aborigens of Malta.

Several other quotations from Cicero, and particularly from Homer, who mentions the island under the name of Ogygia, together with the preceding, if not decisive proof, go far to establish the early settlement of the Phœnicians in Malta.

The argument adduced by some to confirm this, from the vernacular language of the country, is as altogether unnecessary as it is uncer-

(*) Diod. Sic. Lib. V. c. I.

tain. The several words which have been brought forward as Punic, may all be traced back to an Arabic original; and in fact the very small knowledge which we have of this ancient language, hinders us from drawing any satisfactory conclusions from such a comparison. The Rev. Mr. Schlienz, in his late treatise on the "Use of the Maltese language for the purposes of Education and Literature," p. 38. very clearly shows, that we have no certain criterion to guide us in ascertaining the Phœnician character of the Maltese language.

In the hall of the Public Library are still preserved three medals with Phœnician inscriptions, as well as two other monuments of the same language. If I may be permitted to advance the opinion, I should say, that the sepulchral grots in the mountains of Bengemma, are also remains of the work of this ancient people. Any person who has visited the region of Tyre and Sidon, the early seat of the Phœnician kingdom and seen those which still exist there in abundance, will be struck at once with the analogy between them, both as to the manner in which they are excavated, and the position in which they lie.

From the various medals and other monuments which have been found in this island, as well as from the accounts of ancient history, it appears that the Greeks held possession of it for some time after their expulsion of the Phœ-

nicians. According to Thucydides and Syco-
phoron (*), the arrival of the Greeks in Malta
ought to be dated after the Siege of Troy, in
the first year of the second Olympiad, 755 years
B. C. After that famous expedition, which
has immortalized the muse of Homer, part of
the confederated Greeks returned to their native country, while the remainder sailed for
that part of Italy, which is called Calabria,
where they founded the cities of Crotone and
Taranto, and many other colonies. From this
they sailed to Sicily where they built Syracuse
and Agrigentum, and then scattered themselves
over the islands of the Mediterranean. They
chased the Phœnicians from Malta, which at
the period was called Ogygia, changed the
name into Melitas, and established here their
own form of government.

Cicero (contra Verres, lib. IV.) speaks of the
Temple of Juno, belonging to the Greeks at
Malta as being very splendid, and situated not
far from the Great Harbour. The worship of
the goddess, most probably existed here in the
time of the Phœnicians (as may be inferred
from a medal in the Public Library), by whom
she was worshipped under the title of Iside.
The learned Abela in his *Malta Illustrata*, lib.
ii. not. v. accumulates evidence to prove the domination of the Greeks in this island, and the

---

(*) See Thucid. lib. viii. Sycoph. Cassand. lin. 1627.

flourishing state of commerce during their government.

In the year of the world 3620, the Carthaginians who had settled themselves along the
northern coast of Africa, and had seized upon
several islands in the Mediterranean, attacked
Malta and Sicily under the conduct of Hannibal, and made themselves masters of it. It was
however, not without much effort and bloodshed
that they succeeded, as the Greeks were continually sending reinforcements from Sicily to
the assistance of the island. The conquerors
treated the inhabitants with great lenity, ac-
corded to them the free practice of their own
religion, and laws, and in short time, rendered
their circumstances more flourishing than ever.

From several inscriptions, which have been
found here, the fact may be established beyond
dispute, that this ancient people flourished here
at a very early period. A square stone, with
an inscription in Punic characters, discovered
in a sepulchral cave near the place called Ben-
Ghisà, on which Sir W. Drummond has written
a learned essay, is supposed to mark the burial-
place of the famous Carthaginian general Hannibal. This is a curious piece and one of the
largest remains of the Punic language now in
existence; and as it helps to ascertain the ancient inhabitants of this island I think it not
improper to insert the translation.

THE INNER CHAMBER
OF THE SANCTUARY OF THE SEPULCHRE
OF HANNIBAL,
ILLUSTRIOUS IN THE CONSUMMATION
OF CALAMITY,
HE WAS BELOVED;
THE PEOPLE LAMENT, WHEN ARRAYED
IN ORDER OF BATTLE,
HANNIBAL THE SON OF BAR-MELEC.

To such a thriving condition did Malta arrive
during the government of the Carthaginians,
that it became an object for the ambitious cupi-
dity of the Roman power, after the termination
of the first Punic war. Twice was the island
pillaged; the first time by the Consul Attilius
Regulus, and afterwards by Cajus Cornelius.
Finally, it fell into the hands of the Romans,
together with the island of Sicily, under the
Consul Titus Sempronius, at the commencement
of the second Punic war.

By order of the senate, Malta was declared a
Roman municipality; a prefect was appointed
over it, who was subject to the pretor of Sicily
and Marcus Marcellus was ordered to fortify
this port, so important for the defence of Sicily
and the whole of Italy. The Romans neglected
nothing in order to conciliate the inhabitants,
who were strongly attached to the Carthaginians by a common origin and language. They
respected their laws, encouraged the manufac-
tories which they found established, and partic-

ularly that of the cotton, which was so renowned that Cicero informs us, it was regarded as a luxury even at Rome. Besides all this, the Maltese people were permitted to coin money in their own name, to govern themselves by their own laws, to administer justice, to enjoy the right of suffrage in the Roman council, were eligible to any office in the Republic and permitted to present offers to Jupiter Capitolinus, a privilege the Romans only granted to their nearest allies.

The temples of Hercules and Juno, which existed in this island, and which were objects of veneration to all the people of the East, were very much embellished by the Romans. They also raised a magnificent temple to Apollo, and another to Proserpine, and a theatre, of which some scattered remains of chapiters and pillars are to be seen about the Città Notabile, where they stood.

Many Roman medals and coins have been found in the island, and several inscriptions, which prove the privileges enjoyed by the Maltese under that domination. The curious will find lengthened details on this subject in Ciantar's Malta Illustrata, Lib. ii. not. 6.

The Goths who had overrun and made themselves masters of Italy and Sicily, and had pillaged and sacked Carthage, arrived at Malta about the year 506; and after occupying it for thirtyseven years, they were expulsed by

the army of Justinian, under the command of
Belisarius.   In the Public Library, is still to
be seen a monument of the time of the Goths;
and several other inscriptions have occasionally
been met with in the Città Notabile.

The island of Malta now remained under the
dominion of the Emperors of Constantinople,
until the latter part of the ninth century; but
not enjoying the same privileges it had done
in the time of the Romans, the inhabitants did
not attain their former glory.

About the year 879, during the reign of the
Emperor Basil, the Arabs, who had already
overrun all the East, and conquered Spain,
Portugal, Italy and part of France, made a
descent upon the island of Gozo, which they
soon took, and massacred all the Greeks whom
they found in it.   From Gozo they crossed over
to Malta, which nobly resisted for a length of
time, but was at last obliged to yield to superior force.   The fact is, the Greeks who had
followed Belisarius, had by their oppressions,
rendered themselves obnoxious to the inhabitants who were consequently easily brought over
to give assistance to the enemy; hoping that
by changing masters, they might free themselves from their servitude.

The Arabs upon taking possession of the
island, exterminated all the Greeks, and made
slaves of their wives and children.   They, however treated the Maltese with every mark of

respect, and allowed them the free exercise of their own religion. The Arabs soon found the importance and the advantages which the safe ports of the island afforded to their piratical expeditions, and in order to defend the entrance into the great harbour, erected a fort on the present site of St. Angelo, to secure their vessels from danger of attack. They also added new fortifications around the Cittá Notabile, by them called Medina, and diminished the extent of the walls, in order to facilitate its defence.

During the reigns of the Emperors Nicephorus Phocas and Michael Paphlagonien, an expedition was fitted out in order to expel the Arabs from the island of Malta; on account of their continual piratical excursions upon Italy, and the whole eastern empire, which had become quite an annoyance. The admirals Nicetas and Manianes were appointed to command this enterprise. All their measures however, were disconcerted; for, being incapable of resisting the courage of their enemies, they were obliged to betake themselves to a disgraceful flight.

The most extensive relic preserved in Malta of the domination of the Arabs, is their language. Ciantar gives a very plausible reason why this tongue got such an ascendancy in the island. He says; "As soon as the news was made known that the Saracens had passed over to Sicily with a great military armament, the

most opulent and powerful men of our island
fled to Constantinople, under which government they were." Only the poorer classes remaining behind, they found it almost indispen-
sable to accomodate themselves to the language
of their masters which became their own in the
course of the two centuries they were governed
by them. As a dialect of the Arabic, the present Maltese spoken at Gozo, and in the casals
of Malta, is nearly as good as that of any other
Arabic country ; and it is sad to observe how
little it is appreciated by the people. With a
little cultivation, the Maltese might possess a
written language, which would yield to none in
the beauty of its phrases, or the extent of its
vocabulary. The advantages which would accrue
to the island from a cultivation of the classical
Arabic, is ably demonstrated in the late work
of the Rev. Mr. Schlienz, already alluded to.

After the Arabs had remained in quiet possession of the island for 220 years, Count Roger, son of the celebrated Tancrede de Haute-
ville, in company with his brother William,
expelled them from Malta, as also from Sicily
and Naples, and the neighbouring country.
This event took place about the year 1090. The
inhabitants of these islands regarded Roger as
their deliverer, and as a testimonial of their gratitude, proposed to name him their sovereign.
Roger accepted of the offer, and was accordingly crowned King of Sicily and Malta, in

spite of the opposition of the Pope, and the claims of the Emperor of Constantinople. Michael Comnenus, however, determined to reinstate his power in the islands of the Mediterranean, fitted out two formidable fleets, and committed them to the command of Alexis Comnenus, and Constantine Angelo; but their expedition failed of success, for both were taken prisoners by Roger, who, in order to revenge the outrage, carried his arms into the Emperor's dominions, and returned laden with the spoil of Thebes and Corinth, after having obliged Michael to acknowledge his independence, and the legitimacy of his rights.

Roger, following the spirit of the age, founded and enriched many churches at Malta and made some efforts towards the conversion of the Arabs to the Christian faith. To those, whom he had permitted to remain in his kingdom, he acted with the greatest generosity, and only levied from them a trifling yearly tribute as a sign of their subjection. So far did his toleration extend, that he permitted them to stamp a small gold coin, with the Arabic epigraph: *There is only one God and Mohummed is the Prophet of God.* on one side, and on the reverse, *King Roger.* Some of those coins are still preserved in the private museum of Cardinal Borgia at Villetri.

Notwithstanding, however, the mildness with which Roger treated the Arabs who chose

to remain in the island, they occasionally re-
volted against his authority. In 1120, such of
them as occupied the district called *Kalat-el-
Bahria* attempted to massacre the principal
inhabitants of the island; which obliged the
king to send his son to Malta, in order to
chastise the rebels as traitors to the government.

After the death of Roger II. Costance his
only daughter, who had espoused the Emperor
Henry VI. ceded the islands of Malta and Sicily to the dominion of the Emperors of Germany, of the house of Swabia, notwithstanding
the opposition of Tancrede, the natural son of
her father, who had saized upon the throne.

The death of Tancrede, however, and that of
his unfortunate son, restored peace to the
kingdom, and brought back to the party of
Costance these of the barons whose dislike for
a foreign prince had hitherto caused them to
take sides against her.

Under the government of Henry VI. and of
his son Frederic II. the Maltese greatly signalized themselves by their valour at sea. Under
one of their own Admirals, they attacked and
destroyed a squadron of the Republic of Pisa,
which had come to lay siege to Syracuse; and
took the island of Candia from the Venetians,
after having shattered their fleet, and taken
prisoner their Admiral Andrea Dandalo.

After Malta remained for seventy-two years
under the German Emperors; Manfred, the na-

natural son of Frederic II. formed the horrible design of poisoning his father, and making himself master of his dominions. The cruel oppression and tyrannical proceedings of this usurpur, excited a rebellion of the Maltese and Sicilians against his government, and finally caused Pope Urban IV. to solve all his subjects from their allegiance to him. To avert the consequences of such powerful opposition, he offered his daughter Costance in marriage to Peter, son of James, King of Arragon. This alliance, however, had no other effect upon Urban than that of completing his enmity towards Manfred; and without any right, except that presumptiously assumed by his predecessors, he invested Charles of Anjou, king of France, with the possession of Sicily and Naples, and their depending states. This proceeding was unjustly confirmed by his successor Clement IV. who reserved to himself the duchies of Benevento and Ponte-Corvo, in the kingdom of Naples, and a yearly tribute of forty thousand crowns, which Charles obliged himself to pay to the Papal See on St Peter's day.

A battle which took place between the forces of Charles and Manfred, on the plains of Benevento, on the 26th February, 1266, decided the fate of the kingdom in favour of the former. Manfred met the just punishment of his parricide and other crimes, by being slain on the field, and his family taken prisoners by the conqueror.

In the mean time, Corradin, the legitimate son of Frederic II. and rightful heir to the crown, who was at this period sixteen years old, in company with the duke of Austria pepared to rescue his father's dominions from the hands of Charles. After various successes, they penetrated as far as the town of Aquila in the Abruzzi, where a battle was fought on the plain of Lis, close by the lake of Celano, in the year 1268. The troops of Corradin, being chiefly recruits composed of different nations and fatigued by long marches, could not resist the impetuosity of the French soldiery, and so were obliged to yield. The Duke of Austria, toghether with Corradin, were beheaded in the market-place at Naples, and with the latter the ancient house of Suabia became extinct.

The daughter of Manfred, whose husband was now king of Arragon with the title of Peter III., used all her influence to inspire him to assert his claims to the kingdom of Sicily and Malta. The tyranny of Charles had already rendered him obnoxious to the people whom he governed, and it was not long before a desperate attempt was formed by a private Sicilian gentleman, who was secretely attached to Peter, to massacre all the French in the kingdom at a given signal. This famous conspiracy, known by the name of the *Sicilian Vespers*, was carried into effect on Easter-day of the year 1282, after which the King of Arragon was proclaimed sovereign of Sicily, and publicly crowned in the Cathedral of Palermo,

Charles was in Tuscany when the news of this tragical event reached him. He immediately set about making endeavours to regain his authority; but his fleet, commanded by his son was, discomfited by Admiral Roger, who commanded the vessels of the Arragonese. After this, Roger steered towards Malta, which at that time was governed for the French by William Corner, who had a squadron under his command lying in the harbour. After a bloody engagement, with much loss on both sides, the French commander was obliged to capitulate, and thus the island came under the dominion of the Arragonese.

The island of Malta, after having suffered so much from the dissensions of its successive masters, was now destined to undergo even worse treatment, from the individuals to whom it was successively given as a fief by the Kings of Arragon and Castile. Notwithstanding the solemn promises made by King Louis, son of Peter II. at the just and urgent representations of the Maltese, that the island should in future be considered as unlienable from the crown of Sicily, it was twice afterwards mortgaged by King Martin; first to Don Antonio Cordova, and subsequently to Don Gonsalvo Monroi, for the sum of 30,000 florins.

Oppressed out of measure with the grevious

yoke which they had to endure under these circumstances, and wearied of making useless complaints, the Maltese resolved to pay to Martin the sum of which the island had been pledged. This generous offer was accepted, and in the year 1350, by a public act of the king, it was decreed that the islands of Malta and Gozo should henceforth never be separated from the kingdom of Sicily; and that their inhabitants should enjoy equal privileges, with those of Palermo, Messina, and Catania.

In 1516, this entire kingdom passed into the hands of Charles V. of Germany, the heir of all the Spanish dominions. Notwithstanding his confirmation of the previous declaration of his predecessors, concerning the perpetual junction of Malta with Sicily; this emperor, for political reasons, resolved to cede the islands to the Order of St. John of Jerusalem, the remains of which were at the time at Viterbo, in the Papal States. The act of the donation is dated at Castel Franco, near Bologna, March 23, 1530; and the document of the acceptance of the gift, by the council of the Order, April 25th, of the same year. The substance of the act was as follows: That the Emperor Charles V. King of Sicily, gave to the Order of St. John of Jerusalem, in his name, and in that of his successors, the islands of Malta, Gozo, Comino, and Tripoli in Africa, as a free and noble fief, with all the privileges of sovereignty, under these conditions:

1. That every year the Order should present a falcon to the King, or Viceroy of Sicily.

2. That the bishopric of Malta should always be nominated by the king.

3. That the chief admiral of the fleet should always be an Italian.

4. That they should preserve to the Maltese all their rights and privileges.

The Grandmaster having accepted these conditions, embarked to take possession of the island, where he arrived on the 26th of October 1530, accompanied by a great many knights and principal officers of the Order. The Maltese at first, were by no means pleased at the change, which they considered as an infringement upon their engagemet with the King of Sicily; but, being assured by the Emperor, that their privileges would be religiously preserved to them by the new government, they quietly submitted.

The first care of the knights, after having settled their authority through the two islands, was to provide some better accommodation for the present, and to choose a proper place to fix their future habitation. But, as the island had no other defence than the old castle of St. Angelo, and was so much exposed on all sides, that it would have required greater sums than their exhausted treasury could spare to put it in a proper state to resist an attack, the Grandmaster was obliged to content himself with

surrounding the above mentioned castle, (wherein he had ordered new buildings to be reared
for the present habitation of his knights) with
a stout wall, to prevent its being surprised by
the Turkish and Barbary corsairs.

The Turks made several attempts to gain a
footing on the island; but were always repulsed
with loss. In 1546, the famous Corsair Dragut
effected a landing, and sacked the village Tarscien; but being attacked by the English commander Upton, at the head of the Maltese, he
was obliged to betake himself to a disgraceful
flight. In 1551, another attempt was made,
which proved equally unsuccessful to the Turks;
but in which the Order lost the Cavalier Repton,
the Grand Prior of England. D' Omedes, who
was Grandmaster at this time, added a great
many fortifications to the island. Claude de la
Sengle, his successor, carried on these means of
defence, especially the walls around the peninsula, which is now called after his name, La
Sengle, or Senglea.

During the reign of John de la Valette, who
succeeded La Sengle, Malta was destined to
undergo its severest attack from the hands of
the Turks. A short sketch of the siege and the
capture of the castle St. Elmo will be given
under the description of that fort, which was
the only place the enemy succeeded in taking.
After two successive attempts, the united forces
under Mustapha and Dragut were obliged to

set sail from the island, after suffering great loss, and giving the Knights of Malta an opportunity of testing their renowned bravery and signaled courage.

One of the first care of the Grandmaster, after repairing the fort, which had greately suffered during the siege, was to enlarge the castle of St. Elmo, as this was the chief key of the two ports. But his great design was that of building a new city on the peninsula where it stood, and of fortifying it in such a manner, as might render it a more secure retreat for the Order than that of Borgo, which is commanded by rocks and eminencies. As soon as he had secured sufficient assistance, he immediately set about procuring the best engineers for the enterprise; workmen and materials were brought from Sicily, and he was enabled to lay the first stone of the new city, on the 28th day of March 1566. In 1571, three years after the death of La Valette, the city was completed by the Grandmaster Peter del Ponte, and from that time became the seat of the government.

The successive Grandmaster of the Order augmented the fortifications which had been begun under La Valette, raised numerous forts in the interior, and along the coast of the island, and established various institutions, which will be described in the sequel of this work. A predatory warfare, by sea and land, was continually kept up between the knights of Malta and the

Turks, in which the former generally displayed more valour than true christian charity. They were in general successful, and at length became quite a terror to the Ottoman power.

During the Grandmastership of Emmanuel Pinto, the King of Sicily made some pretensions of the island of Malta, declaring that it had only been yielded up to the Order, on condition that the supreme sovereignty should continue to be vested in the hands of the Kings of Sicily; that consequently he intended to send a Court to the island, called *Monarchia* which should have the jurisdiction over all public affairs. This message was considered an infringement upon the rights of the existing government, and treated with that indignity which so false an assertion merited. Still the king persisted in his attempt, and went so far, as to send the threatened court in a splendid barge, handsomely damasked on the inside, to establish themselves in the island. Hearing of the arrival of so extraordinary an embassy, the Grandmaster sent forthwith to demand their errand; and not less astonished than enraged, when he understood that it was the *Monarchia* he immediately ordered them to leave the harbour, and declaring that in case they disobeyed, he would honour them with a salute of shot. Not expecting such a reception, the disappointed court weighed anchor, and returned home. When the king heard of the failure of his scheme, he ordered the ports of

Sicily to be closed against all Maltese vessels, and cut off the communication between this island and his dominions. This was a terrible blow to Malta as all her supplies were derived from Sicily; and being at continual war with the Turks, she could procure nothing from Africa. At this crisis, the Grandmaster entered into a truce with the Infidels, in order that the Ottoman Ports might be opened to the Maltese. The Turks gladly accepted the proposal, as it gave them a short reprieve from the uninterupted annoyance which their commerce received from the gallies of the Knights. During this time, the Turks continually brought supplies of every kind to the island; and were so assiduous in their attentions, that they even imported snow during summer, which is so much used here in making refreshments. Acting now as they did in conjuction with the Order, in carrying on an offensive warfare against the King of Sicily, they soon made him feel that he had raised up against himself a formidable enemy, which he was not able to repress. After loosing many of his vessels, which had been seized by one or other of his enemies, he sought for a renewal of the peace, relinquished his unjust claims, and made every possible reparation to the Grandmaster, for the war he had occasioned.

The Bailiff Emmanuel de Rohan, of the language of France, succeeded Ximenes, the successor of Pinto, in the year 1775. One of his

first acts after his elevation was to strengthen
the executive government by the formation of a
regular battalion of infantry, composed promiscuously of Maltese and foreigners; but officered
exclusively by knights.   This step was thought
decidedly   necessary,   if   the   knights   wished
to preserve their   authority;   this plan   was
strenously recommended   by several friendly
powers.   This corps was entrusted with the
keeping of La Valette, and the other important
forts; while a considerable force was also enrolled to guard the open coast.   Several other
efforts were made by the Grandmaster, to revive
the ancient discipline of the Order, a new Code
of municipal laws called *Code of Rohan* was
published,   judicious   alterations   were   carried
into effect in the court of judicature, and additional facilities given to the public education.
Nor, while thus busied in improving the internal administration, did the Grandmaster neglect
the foreign policy of the Order.   In Poland he
obtained the restitution of some ancient possessions, and had new commanderies formed in
Russia and Germany;which latter were endowed with the confiscated property of the Jesuits,
to the extent of £15,000.

This however, was only the sunshine of prosperity, which was destined to be darkened by
the clouds of adversity. Towards the latter
part of Emmanuel de Rohan's reign, the Order
suffered serious losses, by the extinction of

many of its commanderies, and the taxes imposed upon others by their several governments. By an edict of France dated 19th of September 1792, the Order of Malta was declared to be exinct within the French territories, and its possessions were annexed to the national domains. To show the delapidated state of the revenue, it need only be mentioned, that the receipts, which were in 1783 upwards of three millions of livres, were in 1797 reduced to one million. Not only were the possessions of the three French languages confiscated, but the German and Arragonian commanderies, situated in Alsace, Rousillon, and French Navarre, fell also a prey to republic rapacity. Even in Spain, Sicily, Portugal and Naples, a similar system of spoliation had taken place. In this extremity, the Grandmaster Hompesch, who had succeeded Rohan, found it necessary to melt, and coin the plate of the gallies, and part of that used for the service of the hospitals; and to make use of the jewels, which were deposited in the palace and in several of the churches.

The French government, which had for some time manifested a spirit of hostility to the Order, now came forward to display it openly. The first division of the French fleet arrived before the port of Malta, on the 6th of June 1798. On the 9th., General Bonaparte, with the remainder of the squadron, stood off the island, and through his consul Caruson demanded free admission for the whole fleet. This not being complied with, on the same day, towards evening, the French began to disembark at the bay of Maddalena, and carried the small fort of St. George, without the loss of a single life. On the following day, fresh body of troops were thrown ashore, without meeting with any resistance; who immediately, began to lay waste the island with their usual licence. Towards the evening, the French army had secured almost all the important posts in the country, and had advanced beneath the walls of the city, where the greatest uproar now prevailed among the people on account of the treachery which had been discovered among several knights of the Order.

On the 17th a council was called, and it was resolved to yield up the city into the hands of the besiegers. No sooner did the French find themselves the uncontrolled masters of the island, than they enjoined all the knights to quit it within three days. About ten pounds sterling were advanced to each, for travelling expenses; but they were not permitted to depart, until they had torn the cross from their breast, and substituted the three coloured cockade. By the articles of capitulation, the French engaged to pay to the Grandmaster an annual pension of 300,000 livres, and to each French knight resident in Malta, a yearly allowance of 700 livres, with 300 livres additional, to each as exceeded sixty years of age. Hompesch, accompanied by twelve knights, embarked on the night of the 17th of June, on board a merchant ship bound for Trieste, accompanied by a French frigate. This weak man died at Montpelier 1804, in the sixty-second year of his age. The knights who followed the most prosperous course, at the general dispersion, were those who took refuge in the Russian dominions, under the wing of their Imperial protector. The Emperor Paul was solemnly inaugurated, as the seventieth Grandmaster of the Order, in the year 1798; a nominal dignity, for which he had anxiously longed. At the same time, the standard of St. John was hoisted on the bastion of the admiralty at St. Peters-burgh, were it continues· unfurled unto this day.

Paul made several attempts to reorganize the Order, and to this end invited the nobility of Christendom to enlist themselves as knights in its service. A sudden change of policy, however, put an end to his project, for the army which he had raised to act in junction with the English for the reconquest of Malta, was sent to act against the British possessions in the East.

The French expedition, with General Bonaparte, weighed anchor from Malta, on the 19th of June, leaving General Vaubois with 4,000 men for the defence of the island. The rarities found in the public treasury, and in the churches

of the Order, toghether with their standards
and trophies, were all carried away by the
spoilers, but never reached the country for
which they were destined: part of them perished in the *Orient*, which was blown up in the
battle of Aboukir, and the rest were captured
by the English in the frigate *Sensible*, which
afterwards fell into their hands.

In the meanwhile, the Maltese began to feel
that they had exchanged a feeble despotism
for a yoke of extreme rigour. The French soldiery committed all sorts of depredations through
out the city; all faith was violated, every species
of injustice was committed, the pensions suspended, and even the charitable benefactions to
the indigent, which the knights had daily continued to the hour of their surrender, were
withheld. The acts of oppression created an
invincible antipathy in the Maltese for the government of their invaders, and at length produced a sudden burst of popular vengeance.
An attempt was made to despoil the church of
the B. V. Mary of Mount Carmel, of the Città
Notabile, in order that its decorations might be
sold for the public service, whereupon the inhabitants, rendered furious by a proceeding so
sacrilegious, congregated in a body to prevent
the sale. The French commandant Masson
succeeded in partly quelling the tumult, but he
soon found it necessary to apply for fresh troops
from Valetta. Before these could arrive, the

population was reinforced by the villagers of Casal Zebbug who massacred the entire French detachment, with their commander, amounting to sixty men. From this moment, all communication ceased between the city and the interior, and Valetta assumed the aspect of a place reduced to a state of blockade.

Matters were in this state when the English fleet appeared off the island, and in conjunction with a Portuguese squadron held a parley, in which it was demanded that the island should be immediately evacuated. The answer returned was one of defiance, and a rigorous blockade was forthwith commenced. The Portuguese admiral was left alone to maintain the blokade during the temporary absence of the English squadron, on the return of which, a fresh summon was sent for the place to surrender. Early in December the same was repeated, which was firmly and laconically answered. Hitherto the city had only been partially canonaded by a few guns, but on the night succeeding the last refusal, several new batteries were unmasked, and some balls happening to fall within the walls, the inhabitants feared that the threatened bombardment was about beeing put into execution. Famine now began to stare them in the face, and the greatest misery raged amongst the citizens and soldiery. In these circumstances, the inhabitants of the interior planned an enterprise against the garrison, in conjunction with

c

a strong body of the town people, who were involved in the plot, and who were ready to rise in arms, as soon as they should hear the clangour of arms on the battlements. Two hundred Maltese, favoured by the night, crept into the ditches and along the sea shore, close under the city walls in the Marsamuscetto harbour; but while lying in ambush, they were unfortunately discovered, and the alarm was given to the garrison. On this occasion forty-four of the conspirators were apprehended, and shot by the French authorities.

The blockade had now lasted for six months, and the city exhibited a scene of frightful privation. The besiegers would not permit any to leave the town, knowing that their doing so would relieve the garrison. Disease added its ravages to the general suffering, and soldiers and citizens became alike its victims. Month after month passed heavily over, and in August 1800, the citizens being totally beggared, the army was put on half pay. Four months afterwards it was entirely stopped, and their rations greately lessened. Still they bore all with astonishing fortitude, being supported with the hope of a speedy deliverance. At length, however, the news of the interception of the supplies and their capture by the English, disheartened many, though it did not at once decide them to capitulate. The condition of the town was dreadful beyond description. Fresh pork brought seven shillings and two pence a pound; rats sold at an exorbitant price; dogs and cats were generally eated; and horses, asses and mules were similarly converted into articles of food. On the 8th of September 1800, a parley was held with the besiegers, when the terms of capitulation were arranged and ratified by Major general Pigot and Commodore Martin on behalf of the English. On the afternoon of the same day, two English frigates und some small craft entered the port; while the British troops took possession of the Forts Tignè, Ricasoli and Floriana, The following morning the French garrison sailed away, after having endured an obstinate blockade of two years.

According to the treaty of Amiens, concluded in 1802, the island of Malta and its dependencies were to have been restored to the Order of St. John of Jerusalem, but this treaty was never put into execution; war having been again declared between France and England, leaving this latter power in possession of these islands, in accordance with the ample consent and wishes of the Maltese.

In the year 1814, agreable to the resolution of the Congress of Vienna, the islands of Malta, Comino and Gozo were confirmed to the English Crown; and they have ever since been considered, by all the powers of Europe, as a British dependency.

By way of comparison, we shall just give a

succint account of the state of financial affairs
during the last years of the reign of the knights
of Malta, in order to show that the island has
lost nothig in point of wealth or prosperity, in
having ceased to be the conventual residence of
that government, and in having come under the
rule of the British Crown.

Reverting to the public expenditure of the
Order, it may be satisfactory to compare it
with the disbursement made here in present
time out of funds voted by the British parliament.

In the time of the Order the *general* treasury,
which may be said to answer to our *military
chest*, provided for the military and naval charge,
so far corresponding with the supplies now
made by H. M.'s treasury for carrying on similar services on this station.

The money laid out within the place by the
general treasury from the foreign resources of
the Order, on an average of ten years ending
in 1788, did not exceed, if it even amounted to
£ 82,525.

From the *First Report of the Commissioners
of Colonial Inquiery*, 8th December 1830, it is
collected that the disbursement from the revenues of the United Kingdom made within these
islands for the service of the land-force alone,
including the commisariat and ordnance departments, but leaving out the Maltese regiment
(the expense of which is refunded from the local

treasury,) amounted in round numbers to £ 101,000. (*)

Of this sum, it may be inferred from the same Report that about £ 7,000 were expended in England; which will leave £ 94,000 for the local expense, being in round numbers £11,000 more than were laid out in the place from the treasury of the Order of all its services.

To this excess of £ 11,000 must be added the expenses of the naval department in works of masonry, in the repairs and supplies of ships of war, and in payments on account of seamen's wages, all of which have been very considerable of late years, though varying according to circumstances; and it will probably result that, for the lowest year, the expenditure of the United Kingdom in these islands has exceeded by about fifty per cent the corresponding public expense of the Order.

By the same document it is seen that the works and repairs of the ordnance and barrack departments amounted in 1829 to no less a sum than £ 6,390; and, if the extensive works of the naval department be added, it must be evi-

(*) According to the parliamentary return of the military expenses lately laid upon the table of the House of Commons, it appears that the expense of this island to the Military Chest of Great Britain was, for the year ending 31st March 1857, £167,671; only exceeded by the extensive colonies of Jamaica, the West Indies, Canada, New South Wales, and the Cape of Good Hope

dent that the Order cannot approach a comparison with the British government on the score of employment given to the industrious inhabitants.

Besides the expenditure out of the public treasury of the Order, it is assumed, on a generous calculation, that the sum of £ 185,000 was annually put into circulation in the island out of the private incomes of the knights and other members. Against these disbursements are to be set the whole personal expenditure of naval officers, (*) the portion of expense arising from the private incomes of military officers, and the excess of money spent beyond what may have been the case formerly, in consequence of the greater affluence of strangers to the place, under the extended connexions and superior protection now enjoyed through British power and influence.

The last assumption may indeed admit of dispute; but in whatever light it may be viewed, it will remain with the reader to form his own conclusion in regard to the extent to which the island may have obtained compensation, since it has been annexed to the British empire, for loss of the benefit which it derived from the incomes of the resident knights.

It is well known, however, that of late years British squadrons have continued at anchor in

---

(*) That of the seamen, originating from the military chest, comes into the comparison of "public" expenditure.

this port during many successive months. The
money laid out in the place by the officers and
seamen, and expended in the supply of fresh
provisions, is likely to amount, at such times,
for each ship of the line, to between £ 1000 to
£ 2000 a month, exclusive of the charge for
repaires and the supply of stores.

But whatever may have been the effect, to
contest the superior protection enjoyed under
the present ruling power, can scarcely enter
the imagination of one accustomed to judge
from the evidence of his senses. Let him refer
to a map of the island, and he will perceive the
population huddled together within from half
to two-thirds of it surface, and (where not
bounded by precipitous heights and rugged
shores) shut in by lines or works of defence,
such as those at Marsascirocco, St. Julian's,
Nasciar and elsewhere,— works now become
useless, although they still continue to bound
the generally inhabited part of the island,
through the force of habit and the situation of
the parish churches. This concentration was
caused by the insecurity of the people. In the
days of the Order, no inhabitant trusted himself to sleep on the coast unsecured by walls
of defence, as the solitary mansions of Spinola
and Selmoon, built in those times strong enough
to repel a sudden attack of corsairs, fully attest;
but, under British protection, the marine villages of St. Julian's and Sliema have sprung

up, where the inhabitants enjoy the sea-breeze without dread of being dragged from their beds into slavery.

The truth is, that, without the protection of a great maritime power, Malta must be constantly exposed to aggressions, which can only cease or become mitigated in proportion as they reduce her to poverty, and leave her an object of no temptation. The island is not naturally fertile but by the exertions of an industrious population aided by a genial climate it has been rendered highly productive, through the adequate protection enjoyed during the last three centuries. That it was flourishing under the Phœnicians, Greeks, Carthaginians and Romans, the monumental remains would prove, if the facts were not evident from the maritime power of those nations combined with its favorable position; but during the middle ages, under the precarious sway of Arabs, Normans and Sicilians the island fell to decay, and had not recovered in 1530, when it was given over by Charles V. to the knights, who found the place in a state of great destitution. This fact appears from the report of the commissioners who on that occasion were deputed by the knights to visit Malta. Among other remarks they observed: "The island is continually exposed to the rapacity and devastation of infidel corsairs, who, without any dread of the castle, freely enter both ports, and very often reduce

to slavery a great number of poor Maltese."
The population has been estimated (*) to have
consisted at this time of about 25,000 souls in
both islands, and to have increased to about
100,000 during the following 268 years of occupation by the Order. This advancement in
population, and consequently in wealth, could
not have proceeded, had it not been guarded
by the maritime power of the knights, furnished
as it was by the catholic, and respected by the
protestant states of Europe. Previously to their
sway, the two principal harbours seem, by the
extract just given, to have facilitated invasions
rather than afforded defence, and an inner cove
was selected for the sea-ports, but the knights
transferred their main position to the neglected
site on which Valetta now stands between the
two harbours, which in time became no longer
disproportioned to the extent of her commerce
and public establishments.

Nevertheless, the protection of the Order,
superior as it was to anything previously enjoyed by the Maltese, was not of a nature, through
its continued course of warfare with piratical
states, to advance them far as a maritime people. Notwithstanding the advantageous position of the island, in the channel dividing the
eastern from the western portion of the Medi-

(*) Ransijat, "Journal du Siège et Blocus de Malte" p. 295.

terranean, insecurity against depredators at sea
originally forced the Maltese to become a rustic
rather than a maritime people. Under the
knights, the people felt secure, considered as
a single body like a garrison confidently sus-
taining a siege, whose killed, wounded and
captured are not of sufficient number to effect
a marked impression upon the general features
of the place; but under the superior maritime
power of Great Britain, the security is felt by
each individual in his own person.

That there is still much room for improvement in the condition of the lower classes here,
and great distress prevailing among them, is
too evident; but whatever may now be the extent of misery, it may be confidently affirmed
to be less than it was in the time of the knights,
if we merely consider the greater portion of
wheaten bread at present consumed within both
islands. During the last years of the Order
the annual consumption of foreign wheat was
about 43,000 salms or quarters by 100,000 inhabitants; at present it averages about 67,000
among 123,000 souls; giving for each individual 3.96 bushels now against 3.44 formerly,
exclusive of the consumption from the native
harvest, which cannot be less at the present
day. As regards their future welfare, let us
hope that, as the Maltese are an industrious
people, who for their honesty, sobriety and
other excellent qualities will bear a comparison

with any nation upon earth, means may be devised for mitigating the distress which many of them continue to suffer through poverty. The charitable disposition of the welthier classes of Maltese is too well known to require being pointed out; but it may be remarked that an extensive field still remains open to their benevolent exertion, by their uniting for the formation of some well concerted plan, adapted to improve permanently the condition of the lower orders of their fellow countrymen.

According to a statement extracted from the documents of the Land-Revenue Office it is seen that between September 1800 and December 1829 the civil services of these islands were supplied out of the revenues of the United Kingdom with no less an aid than the net amount of £ 668,666. 7s. 2d. sterling. (*)

These remarks conclude the comparison between the expenditure of the Order and that of the United Kingdom, as defrayed in Malta. The civil finances of the island under the British Government for the two years 1836 and 1837 is as follows: in 1836 the revenue was

---

(*) For the foregoing account of the finances of Malta under the Government of the Order of St. John of Jerusalem I am indebted to W. Thornton Esq. by whose kindness I am permitted to extract several paragraphs from his valuable work on the subject, printed at the Government Press 1836 to which I refer the reader for the calculation of those statements, which for the sake of brevity I have assumed.

£ 96,392, 8, 10½, the expenditure £ 89,224,10, 3½ ; and in 1837 the income was £103,142. 1. 4. and the total expenditure £97,497, 1, 6 ¾. The chief part of the revenue is derived from maritime duties and dues, and the proceeds of landed rents belonging to the English crown; the interior taxes on the island last year amounted only to £ 2,858,16,3¼.

Since Malta has been under the dominion of England, the inhabitants have enjoyed all the rights and privileges of British subjects. Until very recently, the direction of all public affairs was vested in the hands of the governor, (*) who is appointed to the office by the Home Government and who was almost always appointed from amongst the list of generals of the Army; but in the year 1847, the Hon. Mr. Richard More O'Ferrall was appointed Civil Governor of these Islands ; with distinct civil attributions to the great satisfaction of the Maltese, and a General was appointed to command the Garrison. In 1851 the Hon. Mr. O'Ferrall having resigned, the Civil Government was vested in the hands of Sir W. Reid. In 1835, His late Majesty, William IV. was graciously pleased to appoint a Council within these his

(*) When the British took possession of the Island, it was stipulated, that the privileges of the Maltese should be preserved and their ancient laws continued.—(They were then, N. B., governed by their ancient laws. Sir A. J. Ball's letter to Mr. Secretary Whindham, dated 28th February, 1807.

possessions, to advise and assist in the administration of the government thereof; which
Council consisted of six persons, exclusive of the
Governor, three of whom were at all times to
be persons holding offices within this island or
its dependencies, and the remaining Members,
persons not holding offices. The Senior Officer
in command of Her Majesty's land forces in
Malta, the Honourable Chief Justice, and the
Chief Secretary to Government were the three
official Members as aforesaid. The three unofficial Members were elected by His Excellen-
cy the Governor, two from out of the chief
landed proprietors and merchants of the island,
being H. M.'s native-born-subjects, and the
third from out of the principal merchants being
british-born-subjects who ought to have been
actually resident for a period of not less than
two years.

The Members of this Her Majesty's Council
enjoyed the freedom of debate and vote, in all
affairs of public concern that were brought under their consideration in Council; and whilst
Members, were authorized to assume the ad-
junctive title of *Honourable*.

Our most gracious Sovereign Queen Victoria,
considering the Maltese as faithful and loyal
subjects of Great Britain, and recognizing the
reasonableness of their claims to a Popular Representation was induced, in the year 1849, to
grant them a reform in the Council of Govern-

ment, a concession long desired, and granted
no doubt, in the full persuasion that their loyal-
ty and prudence, entitled them to such a privilege, as to have direction in all public affairs.

The Council of Government at present consist of eighteen persons, holding offices with
the local government, and not holding offices.
The ten official members nominated by the
Crown are the Governor, the Senior officer in
command of H. M's land forces, the Chief Secretary to Government, the Crown Advocate,
the Collector of Customs, the Superintendent
of Quarantine, the Auditor of the Accounts,
the Collector of Land Revenue, the Government Cashier and the Comptroller of Contracts;
and the eight unofficial members are elected by
the people, and are eligible every five years. The
members enjoy the same privileges, and title
as those of the late Government Council.

" We admit, that H. M.'s government in granting
the concession to the Maltese, did grant them no more
than a simple minority in the Council, and yet we are
inclined to suppose that even this limited concession
would be displeasing to our author, who by his injurious and suspicious remarks wished to set a trap for
ensuring the property, liberty and privileges both of
his Mother Country and of the Maltese people; for, if
the Maltese, in ancient times under the Phœnicians,
Romans, &c. were governed by their own laws and

customs, enjoyed the right of suffrage in the Roman
Councils, were eligible to any office in the Republic
&c. and at present under the British Nation and civilization, though they "are industrious people, who for
their honesty, sobriety and other excellent qualities,
will bear comparison with any nation upon earth," yet
are deemed by our author, unfit to have such an establishment—as the *Consiglio Popolare*, indeed is nothing
but a disgrace to, and even an inconsistency with the
British Constitution, a direct opposition to the stipu-
lation made at the time of placing their Island under
the British protection, and contrary to the sacred promises of H. M.'s representatives communicated to the
Maltese in different Proclamations; "That His Majesty grants you full protection, and the enjoyment of
all your dearest rights. Happy people!"

"But on the contrary we are well persuaded, that
the privilege granted to the Maltese by their gracious
sovereign of choosing a portion of the New Council, is
not meant as a farce to amuse them for a moment and
then to be forgotten, but as an earnest of still greater
concessions at a proper time. From the commencement of the British Government's friendly demonstra-
tions, the same cry of contempt has our author raised,
who for his own private ends, has put himself forward
as the pretended champion of the Malta Religious Reformation. When the trial by Jury was instituted, it
was with him all a *farce* for Malta and yet we fearlessly
assert that no country into which it has been introduced, appreciated its value, or understood its routine

sooner than the Maltese. When the liberty of the press was granted, the same cry was heard from him. —*What liberty of the press? The Ordinance is destructive to that liberty which the law is bound to protect; in Malta we want something else than such a shakkled press.* It came into operation however, and has gone on for many years with as much credit and satisfaction as in any Country that ever enjoyed the privilege; and so we confidently affirm, the still greater privilege which has now been conferred on the Maltese, as loyal a people as any connected with Great Britain."

In the year 1836 in consequence of a petition from the Maltese to the House of Commons, a Royal commission of Enquiry was appointed to examine into the affairs of the Island, consisting of two eminent gentlemen, Mr. J. Austin and Mr. George Cornewell Lewis, who resided in the Island for about eighteen months, during which time many alterations and reforms were made in the local administrations. Freedom of the press was amongst the first objects that occupied their attention. The censorship was abolished and an ordinance in Council was promulgated on the 14th March 1839, to that effect, under some provisions against abuses of the liberty of publishing printed writings. Consequently many journals and periodicals were published the greater number of which ceased after a miserable lingering existence, but the

Portafoglio Maltese, the *Mediterraneo,* the *Malta Times* and the *Ordine* have held on and promise to continue in their present flourishing condition.—Many changes were effected in Customs and other Dues, duties on goods for transhipment were suppressed, and moderate fixed dues were established on eight articles of necessity and general consumption, thereby insuring a fixed revenue to Government. The Charitable Institutions were reorganized, several sinecure situations suppressed, departments united, exorbitant salaries diminished and natives declared eligible to occupy all public situations from which they had before been *de facto* excluded— The only situations reserved for Englishmen were those of Chief Secretary, First Assistant Secretary and Auditor of Accounts.—Primary Instruction was reorganized under a more efficient system, and several schools were opened in the country districts. The judicial departments were remodeled and rendered more simple and the Interior Police augmented and established on the same footing as the English Police.

PART SECOND

GENERAL DESCRIPTION

OF MALTA.

PART SECOND.

DESCRIPTION OF MALTA.

TOGETHER WITH A BRIEF OUTLINE
OF ITS PRODUCTIONS, CLIMATE, LANGUAGE, &c.

Geographical situation and features of the Island.

MALTA, in respect to its situation, is farther distant from the mainland than any other island in the Mediterranean. It lies in 35º 50 of north latitude, and 14º .12 east longitude from Greenwich. It is 60 miles distant from the nearest point of Sicily, which bounds it on its north between Capo Passaro and Camarano; 190 miles from Cape Spartivento, the nearest point of mainland of Italy, and 200 from Calipia, the nearest point of Africa; so that by its position, it may claim to be an island appartaining to Europe. It is about 60 miles in circumference; its greatest width is twelve, and length twenty. Its longest day is 14 hours, and 52½ minutes.

The two chief parts of the island are divided by the oblong peninsula on which the town of Valetta is built. The Grand Harbour, which is to the east, was about a mile and a half in length, and less than three quarters of a mile in width at the mouth. This again contains several convenient creeks or small bays, where even large vessels of war may ride safely at anchor.

In the year 1859, this harbour was considerably extended at its head at the Marsa. Its waters are now divided between the Imperial Navy and merchant Shipping, the so called French Creek having been assigned to the former, and the anchorage for mercantile Shipping and private yards having been transferred to the new N. W. Basin. An extensive dock for the use of H. M.'s Navy has been lately contructed in the French Creek in connection with the other Dock which had been formed on the site of the old yard of the Order. Vast and commodious wharves have also been constructed in the new harbour extension, surrounded by stores and other buildings requisite for commerce.

The entrance into this harbour is defended by the forts St. Elmo, Ricasoli, and the castle St. Angelo, so that a forcible landing from this quarter would be next to impossible, if the above fortresses were properly supplied with men and ammunition.

These fortresses are in connection with the batteries of the two *Barraccas* and Fort Lascaris, lately constructed on the site, where the belvidere of the villa of the Grandmasters formerly was.

The harbour to the west, called Marsamuscetto, is destined for vessels arriving from places not in free pratique. Here they are obliged to perform their quarantine, and hence called also the Quarantine Harbour. This latter is also defended by Fort St. Elmo on the one side, and Fort Tignè on the other. The Fort Manoel, which is built on a small island within the harbour, is also intended to act upon its entrance in case of attack.

Besides the harbour above mentioned, there are several others in different parts of the island. The principal of these are Marsa Scala, Marsa Scirocco, Bir - Zebbugia and Saint Thomas's bay on the south-east, and the Bay of St. Paul, St. Julian and Melleha on the north-west. Each of these is defended by a small fort, garrisoned at present by a detachment of the Malta Fencibles. Besides these forts, there are several others built round the coast, in order to prevent smuggling, and to give the alarm in case of the appearance af an enemy off the island.

Around these creeks where formerly only very few buildings were to be seen, fine buildings have been raised, and villages formed, the principal of which are those of Sliema, St. Julians, Melleha, Marsascala and Bir-Zebbugia. With the exception of this last one, which is of more recent formation than the others, these villages are inhabited by a fixed population besides that residing there during the summer months.

Most of the southern coast of the island is by nature inaccessible. The rocks, rising up perpendicularly from the sea to the height of three hundred feet, form a natural fortification, which, it would be impossible to destroy. From the general broken and rugged appearance of many parts of the shore, especially in this quarter, it is very probable that at some distant period the island underwent several extraordinary convulsions of nature; but the occasion of such an event is probably beyond the reach of history or tradition. The other divisions of the coast are low and rocky, and present a very barren appearance.

FERTILITY and PRODUCTIONS.

Soil—Cultivation—Industry of the inhabitants—Corn—Cotton—Clover—Fruits—Figs—Singular process in cultivation of—Supply of water—Cattle—Foul—Birds—Fish.

Notwithstanding the stony soil of Malta the culture wich is bestowed upon it renders it very fertile. The mould is not remarkably rich nor very deep in any part of the island. On many of the hills and rising grounds the fields are enclosed by stony walls, built up so as to form terraces, in order to prevent the heavy rains of winter from washing away the soil, and preventing the cattle from entering them. These walls, which are formed of the broken stones from the quarries of the island, give the country a very monotonous appearance; while their bright colour reflects back the rays of the sun in summer, and renders the heat much more powerful.

The chief productions of the island are corn and cotton. In some parts the land yields 40 and even 60 to one of the former while in others not more than from 12 to 25. This fertility must be attributed as well to the industry of the Maltese farmers, as to the natural richness of the soil. Indeed, the industry of the country people in cultivating their little island is surprising. The land is never permitted to rest, but is laboured and sown year after year without intermission. Wheat is sown every alternate year with barley and clover about the month of November; the harvest commences in June. The barley is gathered about the Month of May. After this crop, the fields are sown with cotton, melons, cummin, sesam, and and other seeds. By this process, the land is not exhausted, and should it appear to be getting poor, instead of barley, peas, beans, Indiancorn other leguminous plants are substituted.

The cotton of Malta is of a very fine quality, and forms the chief article of export. It is of two kinds, distinguished by their colours, one being white, and the other of a dark nankeen colour. This plant is sown about the end of

D

May, and gathered in the yearly part of September when the rains begin. In the year 1801,
the value of raw cotton produced in these islands
amounted to about half a million sterling. From
various causes, however, especially the new
discoveries of machinery for preparing this article, and the abundant supplies from Egypt,
from whence it can he procured at a cheaper
rate, the value is fluctuating. During the recent Civil War in America, its price attained
an unusual figure, from which fact the agricultural class derived considerable profits. The
seed of this plant is used by the inhabitants for
fattening their cattle, and I remarked that the
same custom prevailed in the east, it being the
chief food which the Arabs of Syria and Pales-
tine give to their camels.

A fine species of clover, called by Linnæus
"hedysarium coronarium" with a red flower, is
very abundantly produced in this island during
the rainy season. The appearance of the fields
when this plant is in blossom is really delightful. It grows to the height of from four to five
feet, and forms green forage for horses, mules,
&c. in winter, and what remains is put up and
dried to be used as hay in summer. The other
provendor given to cattle is barley and carobs:
both which are raised in the island, but not in
sufficient quantity for the consumption. The
carob or locust abounds here, and is one of the
few trees which are green all the year round.

It is found scattered about the country, and grows in the most stony and rocky soil. Many of the poorer classes use this fruit as an article of food, and when baked in the oven possesses by no means a disagreeable flavour.

Besides the above, Malta affords a great abundance of vegetables and fruits. In fact, it would be a surprising sight for a stranger to stand without the gates of Porte des Bombes, before sun-rise during the fruit season, and see the numerous carts laden with rich supplies of the above articles waiting for admittance into the city.

The market, at this time, is well stocked with strawberries, figs, pomegranates, grapes, apples, pears, peaches, nectarines, apricots, plums, melons, and prickley-pears, which are sold at very low prices, and upon which many of the poorer classes, who are unable to purchase other food, chiefly subsist. The oranges of Malta are justly prized for their excellent quality; and the great quantities which are exported to England and other countries, show the esteem in which they are held abroad. The season continues for upwards of five months, from November to April, during which time these beautiful trees are covered with abundance of fruit. The *egg* and *blood* oranges, and the so-called *Mandarins* are considered the most superior. The former has been produced according to some, by ingrafting the common orange bud on a pomegranate stock; but this opinion is quite unnatural, and requires evidence to sustain it. The grapes also are excellent, but the island does not produce more than sufficient for its own consumption. A large quantity of vines were destroyed after the repeal of the law of 1838 on the subject of the distillation of spirits. The first fig, which is called *baitra ta San Juan* or St. John's fig, because is generally ripe about the anniversary of the feast of that saint, is of a large size, much larger than I ever met with in any part of the East. About the latter end of July, three other kinds appear, of a smaller size, but of a more delicious flavour; one of these is white, and the other two are of a black or dark purple colour called by the natives *farketsan* and *parsott*. A little later, a second crop from the tree of the first large fig is ripe; but this is of an inferior quality and not held in much esteem.

It is to be observed that the fruit of the country, being the produce of a vegetation growing on an arid soils, is more succous and savoury than that of any other damper region. The melons and pears of Malta are justly held in much esteem.

A peculiar process in the treatment of this fruit is worthy of remark; and the necessity of its adoption in some countries, to the exclusion of others, is a question which the curious may find it interesting to determine. When the figs are advancing towards maturity, in order to prevent their falling off, and to hasten the ripening, a cluster of male figs is suspended upon the branches of the female tree, by means of a plant (Ammi majus) called on this account *Dakra*, which effectually secures them from the danger, and soon effects the desired end. The male tree is called by the natives *dokkara*; and so many small winged insects are generally found in the fruit upon opening it, is the firm belief of the country people that the tree generates them. I have heard several opinions advanced on the subject, but the most rational way of accounting for it, is, that these small flies, which abound about all kinds of fruit trees, entering into the male fig, get clothed with the pollen with which the stamina on the inside is covered, and, carrying it with them into the female fig, produce that natural condition which is necessary for the effectual generation of fruit.

Attempts were made during the government of Sir Fred. Cavendish Ponsonby to cultivate the cochineal in these islands; but the attempt failed, as the climate was not found to be favourable. More recently, also much has been done in regard to the rearing of silk-worms for which numerous trees were planted during the government of the late Marquis of Hastings; but, although the silk produced was of an excellent quality, it was found that the trade would not turn to profit, as the worms did not thrive, and has therefore lately been abandoned.

The land is supplied with water by the various wells and springs which are found on the island.

The spring-water is derived from about 80 springs of different sizes. The principal of them are received into two Aqueducts which supply water to the towns at an average rate of not less than 500 Imperial gallons per minute.

Of the latter there are a great many, besides numerous cisterns in almost every field throughout the country. These together with the night dews which fall during the spring and summer months are sufficient to render the ground fertile and abundant, because the soil, being very shallow, is soon moistened through; and as the rock below is of a soft porous nature, it retains what is over and thus keeps the roots perpetually moist. Were this not the case, there would be no crops at all in summer, the heat of the sun being so exceedingly violent.

In regard to cattle, the greater part of the consumption of the island is brought over from the Barbary States. Oxen, especially, are imported from that quarter, and after being fed here for a short time yield very excellent beef. The mutton is less valued, as it is much poorer on account of the little pasture there is for cattle in the country. The sheep, however, are very prolific, often bringing forth four lambs, and scarcely ever less than two. The goats are of a superior quality, very large, and yielding abundance of milk. It is the custom for the milk-man to lead about his goats in the morning and evening through the streets, in order to serve any who call for him; he then kneels down at the door, and milks, the animal before the customer. The milk of sheep is used particularly for making curd; and in Gozo, a very pleasant kind of fresh cheese, with which it supplies our island, is produced from the same.

The asses and mules of Malta and Gozo are very remarkable for their extraordinary size and the symmetry of shape. These animals form the chief vehicles for carrying burdens and for draught, and not unfrequently are seen yoked with oxen engaged in treading out corn. The Maltese are in general very careful of their beasts, and take care to supply them with a sufficiency of food.

The race of Maltese dogs, so much renowned in Europe, and called *bichons* by Buffon in his Natural History, is now nearly extinct. They are very small, with long glistening hair reaching down to the feet, a face covered with the same, and a turned up nose. I acknowledge that I can see but very little beauty in these dwarfish creatures, and am led to think it is only their rarity which fixes their value at so high a price; they are sometimes sold for forty dollars.

Fowls, turkies, ducks, geese, rabbits and other domestic birds and animals are always found in the market, though not of a very superior quality. Game is less plentiful, except in the months of September and April, when there are generally a great many quales, which light upon the island in their flight, and are not unfrequently caught by the hand. Wild duck, snipes, fig-peckers, woodcocks, plovers and doves form the chief game for sportsmen.

A worthy Governor of these Islands, the late Sir William Reid, had, in the year 1851, instituted Agricultural Exhibitions to be held at the Boschetto on the popular festival of St. Peter and St. Paul, with the view of promoting the agricultural industry and productions of the country. This Exhibition, which is still held annually, is conducted by the Agricultural Society, an institution, which by means of instruction and the distribuiton of prizes, has greatly improved local Agriculture and increased the productions of the country. Another annual exhibition for Floriculture is also held by the same Society at the Upper Barracca in Valletta.

The harbour and the surrounding sea yield abundance of fish, of which there is seldom any want. Mullet, whitings, tunny, sword fish, eels and various others of the crustaceous genus, such as lobsters, crabs and shrimps are the principal supply of the market. Of the testaceous kind, oysters are found in great plenty, as also several species of the *cardium* or cockle, the *venus* the *tellina*, and the *patella*, of which the natives are very fond.

The *phola daetylus* or sea-date, is also another species very much esteemed by the inhabitants. It is found in soft lime-stones taken out of the sea, and in such quantities, that I have seen fifty extracted from a stone not more than a foot square. It is of two kinds, one with a brown and the other with a white shell; the latter is very phosphoric. The late signor Gaetano Trapani, a Maltese gentleman, has published a very interesting catalogue in five languages of the fish to be met with at Malta. He numbers about 150 different species.

In the year 1866, oyster-beds were established in various parts of the coasts for the purpose of ensuring the supply of that testaceous produce.

The *argonauta argo* or Paper Nautilus, is sometimes found here, but I have never seen it together with the animal. The shell is of the *broad keel* species.

BOTANY (*).

The indigenous plants of Malta, or such as grow spontaneously on these islands, are perhaps more numerous than might be expected, from the dry nature of the soil, and the small extent of uncultivated ground existing. Dr. Zerafa, in his FLORÆ MELITENSIS THESAURUS, enumerates 644 species of plants.

Deducting from this number those which are cultivated, and adding the omissions, the whole number of indigenous plants may not perhaps be very far from 700. A great portion of them, as the situation will naturally lead to expect, are maritime plants, common to the Mediterranean in general. Such, however, as require a sandy beach, are comparatively few: as *Polygonum maritimum*, in St. Georges bay; *Cakile Ægyptiacum*, in the bay of Melleha *Euphorbia Peplis, E. Paraliae, E. Terracina*, and *Eryngium maritimum* at Melleha and Gozo; *Pancratium illyricum*, Gozo. One of the most common maritime plants of Malta, and men-

(*) For this interesting article of Botanical production and rarities of Malta, I am indebted to my much esteemed friend Mr. P. Brenner, who has bestowed much attention to his branch of science, particularly as connected with this island. I believe that were he to publish all the information which he has collected on this delightful subject, it would be considered as a valuable acquisition by amateurs.

tioned by Dr. Zerafa, is the lowly *Crucianella maritima*, which blossoms in May and June: the strong aromatic perfume of the flowers of this plant after sunset, betrays it at a distance. On the rock, especially of the southern coast, are particularly to be noticed, *Hypericum, Ægyptiacum*, and *Anthyllis Hermanniae*.

Malta is remarkable for its richness in plants belonging to the natural order *Papillionaceoe*, the *Diadelphia Decandrian* of Linnæus. Of this the genus *Trifolium* counts the greatest number of species, among which the most interesting ones are *T. subterraneum* and *T. suffocatum* both not mentioned by Dr. Zerafa. Then the genuses *Medicago, Melilotus, Lotus*, and *Ononis*. The genus *Duphorbia* contains likewise a considerable number of species. Many different kinds of thistles are met with in Malta of which the most formidable in appearance is the wild artichoke, *Cynara Cardunculus*. Remarkable for its venemous quality is the stalkless and the *Carlina lanata* for its fine purple-coloured flowers. Among the family of the grasses, which Malta contains a great variety, one of the rarest and most curious is *Lygoum spartum*, found at St. Paul's bay, Mtahleb, Fauara, &c. With regard both to abundance and elegance the *Stipa tortilis*, by Dr. Zerafa erroneously called *Stipa pinnata*, is conspicuous. Aromatical plants of the natural class *Labiariflorae*, or *Didynamia, gymnospermia* of Linnæus.

are but few here, as *Mentha Pulegium, Melissa
marifolia, Thymbra hirsuta*. The flowers of the
latter are said to give the Malta honey its peculiar flavour. The plants are gathered and
brought into town in large bundles for fuel.

Owing to the mildness of the climate, there
is no intermission of vegetation all the year
round, and consequently every month produces its peculiar flowers. The beginning of the
vegetable year may justly be counted from the
end of October, when the first rains have begun
to restore to the soil the verdure of winter and
spring. The first and most prominent flower
which then makes its appearance is the *Ran-
nunculus bullatus*, whose broad leaves and fragrant yellow flowers adorn all the uncultivated
ground during November and December. This
is immediately succeeded by the *Bellis annua*,
the white little flowers of which are so abundant in December and January as to make the
hills and way-sides appear as if covered with
snow. Also its much taller sister *Bellis sil-
vestris* is not unfrequently met with at that
season. The chief ornament of spring, however, is the pretty purple flowered *Silene ciliata*
which in March intersperses the white groups
of the Bellis, and gives the ground a most delightful vivacity.

March and April are the months in which vegetation is in its most luxuriant state. Various
species of the natural classes *Ensatae* and

Liliaceæ, or the class *Hexandria* of Linnæus bedeck the fields and hills at this season; as *Asphodelus ramosus, Gladiolus communis, Iris sisrinchium, Narcissus Tazeta, Hyacinthus comosus, Ornithogalum Narbonense,* and *O. Arabicum*; and in May several species of the interesting class *Orchideæ.* The plants which blossom during the summer belong for the most part to the natural class *Compositæ* or *Syngenesia superflua* Linnæi, with yellow flowers, and are almost exclusively maritime plants. For instance, in June and July : *Cineraria maritima, Centaurea Melitensis, Verbascum undulatum* (cl. Labiatifloræ,) *Capparis sativa* (cl. Rhœadeæ) attiring with its large fragrant flowers the walls and rocks of fortifications of Valletta. In July and August : *Inula crithmoides, Crithmum maritimum* (cl. Umbellifloræ). In August and September: *Inula fœtida, Ambrosia maritima, Scilla Maritima,* (cl. Liliaceæ) whose leaves appear in November and die away in May. In September and October: *Inula viscosa,* and *Erigeron graveolens.* A plant very common in Malta, but rare in Europe, is the mean looking *Evax pigmea,* which blossoms in April.

The following plants are confined to particular spots, or are otherwise rare in Malta: *Putoria calabrica,* on a rock in the Uied el Ghasel; *Convolvulus Catabrica,* near Mtahleb ; *Cheranthus tricuspidatus,* near Marsa Scirocco; *Teucrium*

E

Scordioides, Helianthemum Fumana near Gerzuma; *Hyacinthus romanus,* at Fauara, Mtahleb, and Mosta ; *Carthamus coernleus,* at Mtahleb. On the rocks overhanging the Fauara a plant grows plenteously which Dr. Zerafa called *Centaurea spatulatha,* and about which some remarks may be found in the Malta Government Gazette of Feb. 20, 1833. On closer examination, however, it appears that it is no Centaurea. Several German Professors of botany who examined dried specimens did not recognise the plant. It may perhaps finally be made out to be a new genus. In Gozo, the so called General's or Fungus rock, is peculiarly remarkable for various plants not found in other parts of Malta and Gozo. Besides the well known *Cynamorium coccineum* commonly called Fungus Melitensis which blossoms in April and May, there is the *Cheirantus sinuatus, Daucus gummiferus, Gnaphalium ambiguum* and several others. A great variety of sea-weeds are also to be found along the rocky shore (*).

———

(*) See the excellent work on the local Botany lately edited by the learned Prof. G. C. Groch Delicata.

CLIMATE.

The climate of Malta has been variously described by persons, who perhaps were influenced by the particular effects it produced on their individual constitutions. This, though very natural, is an unfair way of deciding the general nature of the climate of any country. The freedom of the island from any endemic. disease, the ordinary good health enjoyed by the natives, by the English, as also by foreigners resident here, and the actual state of the weather throughout the year, go very far towards establishing the salubrious nature of the atmosphere.

During the summer months the thermometer generally shifts from 78º to 84º of Fahrenheit, and towards the end of October sinks, to 70º . From this time it gradually decreases until January, when it varies from 58º to 51º . below which it seldom falls, and again rises about the end of February from 56º to 58º From March to May it generally ascends to 67º , and continues advancing until the latter end of June when the summer sets in.

This range continues from one year to an

other without any important variation (*).

The time however; in which one is most affected by the heat or cold, is not that which marks their extremes on the thermometer. That there is an almost continual contrast between our sensation and the instruments which measure the true temperature of the air, between sensible and real heat and cold, any person who has resided in. Malta for a few years will have discovered. The heat is sometimes very oppressive when the thermometer is comparatively low; and the same remark holds good in regard to the cold in winter, when it is comparatively high. This may be attributed to the direction of the winds, their sudden changes producing a less or greater degree of heat or cold according to the quarter from whence they blow, and their violence modifying the sensations which they cause us to feel. The wind from the north west always brings freshness, while that which blows from the south produces an increase in the heat.

Rain has been known to fall in summer, but is of very rare occurrence. The heat however, is generally tempered by the north and north-westerly winds, which prevail during the hot

(*) The average annual temperature of Malta is 67o. 3. See the able researches " Sulla temperatura dell' Atmosfera in Malta, " 1841. by Dr. Saverio Schembri, Rector of the University of studies.

months, and which render the evening delight-
fully pleasant. Though there are some times
heavy falls of dew during this season, the natives do not find it injurious to sleep out in the
open air, which is quite costumary with many
of the poorer classes, without any bed or covering. When the south wind prevails in summer, the heat is very oppressive : the atmosphere assumes a hazy appearance, the air has
sometimes a disagreeable odour, and its effects
on furniture and book-covers, which it cracks
and warps, are very destructive. After this
wind has lasted for a day or two, the air becomes quite still and confined, and the sensation
felt is exceedingly uncomfortable. It is well
that this state never continues for more than
three or four successive days, and that it is not
of frequent occurrence. This wind, which passes over the arid plains of Africa, is not puri-
fied from the corrupt miasma which it contains
by crossing the sea, as the straits are so narrow
beetween this island and that continent.

The wind, which has procured a bad name
for Malta by foreigners, is the southeast,
usually called the Scirocco. It is most prevalent
in September, yet unfortunately is not confined
to this month alone, but occurs occasionally
throughout the year. Persons with diseased
lungs suffer more or less from its consequences;
and hence Malta is by no means a healthy place
for such as are inclined to consumption.

Strangers, in general, are affected during the prevalence of the Scirocco with great lassitude and debility, which indisposes the system, and renders it liable to suffer from dyspepsia. The natives, however, seldom complain of its bad effects on their constitutions, but more of the inconveniences which it brings to workmen and mechanics. Any thing painted when this wind blows will never set well, glue loses much of its adhesive property, bright metals become tarnished, and from the dampness of the atmosphere the pavement of the streets is sometimes quite wet. Though this wind has occasionally held out for a week together, it seldom last more than three days successively.

The delightful appearance of the evening sky during summer is a phenomenon in the climate of Malta which deserves mentioning. A little before sun-set, and during the interval which elapses between that and dark, the whole western horizon exhibits a beautiful yellow, tinged with a variety of hues, which is truly grand. It is not uncommon for light clouds to intermingle in the scene, and occasionally rapid flashes of lightning to continue for several hours together, which shining beneath the clouds, whose dark edges become more plain from the bright glare imparted to them, and an increasing grandeur to the prospect. Perhaps this sight is not exceeded in magnificence by any appearance in the atmosphere, except the Aurora Borealis of the North.

The winter of Malta is very temperate, though the cold is sometimes exceedingly penetrating. This proceeds from the north wind, which is very prevalent during this season, and by the continued motion which it communicates to the air, incessantly renews the volume of it by which we are surrounded, and causes a sensation of cold which is very acute. That this is the case is proved from the fact, that upon removing from its action, the effects are immediately diminished. The north-east wind, known by the name of Gregale, which blows directly into the mouth of the harbour, has occasionally been sufficiently strong to drive a first rate man - of - war from her moorings. These gales sometimes come on so suddenly, that time is not given to make any provision against them; and consequently it is not an uncommon occurrence for vessels lying at anchor to be injured by the violence of the storm, although the harbour is one of the safest in the Mediterranean.

Rain falls very plenteously here in winter, and occasionally hail, but snow never (*). Very rarely does the rain continue for several days in succession, and it is quite common to enjoy

(*) The annual pluviometrical average is 18 inches. See Professor's G. C. Grech Delicata interesting pluviometrical observation.

delightful clear weather in the coldest season. Storms are not frequent, and then not very violent, although there is in general much thunder during the winter. In cases when the claps are of long duration, and are known by their sound to be in vicinity of the island, all the bells of the churches are made to ring. This however, is generally delayed until the clouds containing the electrical fluid are in the zenith, from which, as it is natural to expect, they soon pass away and with them the lightning and its consequences.

POPULATION.

Number of—Impoverished state of—Cause of the foregoing —Improvidence of the people—Want of education—Bad system of teaching Mechanics—Absence of a spirit of enterprise in the gentry—Character of the people by a Spanish author.

The island of Malta for its size contains a denser population than any other part of the habitable globe. According to this statement it appears that upon a given space of ground where England contains 152 souls, Malta contains nearly eight times the number. The assurance of an easy subsistence is in general considered the most natural cause for the increase of the population of any country; but, in the present case, I do not think the axiom will hold good. Notwithstanding what has been said concerning the fertility of this Island, it is after all only a rock, and incapable from its size to afford adequate means of support to so crowded a population. In these two facts, the disproportionate number of inhabitants to the extent of soil possessed, we must look for the cause of the present impoverished state of the island. It is true that the lack of the produce of a country may be compensated by manufactures and commerce; but of the former Malta has no resources, and her commerce, in spite of every attempt to increase it, remains stationary, and has certainly very materially failed during the last twenty or thirty years. In this respect, however, it is not alone; a general torpor has seized the trading world in this quarter for some time back, the several causes of which I do not intend, as I am unable to explain.

In the report of the late Commissioners sent out to inquire into the grievances of the Maltese, they state the cause of the impoverished condition of the island to arise from " improvidence of the people in multiplying their numbers beyound the demand for their labour. " Nothing can be more true than this fact; no sooner does a lad arrive at the state of puberty, than he begins to think of marriage before he has made any provision at all for maintaining a family. The present system of endowing females is the cause of the most distressing consequences, as in numerous cases it is the only attraction which a young woman has for an individual who seeks her as his wife. However small the sum may be, very few are chosen but such as have something. This, when once in the hands of an idler, is soon spent in some hazardous project or speculation, if not in vice; and when he finds he can procure no more, either from his wife or her relations, he leaves her to her fate, either to be again received under her parents' roof, or to seek a living for herself and family in the best way she can. This is not an exaggerated picture of very many cases in Malta; and besides this, if the computation were made of the number of females at present on the island, whose husbands have left them for a foreign land, I believe it would not fail to astonish.

To the above, however, we may add the want of education as another cause of the poverty of the island. The overplus population which finds an asylum in the Barbary States, in Egypt, Syria, and in Turkey are chiefly of one class, consisting almost exclusively of labourers who have already more than satisfied the demand for their work, and are, consequently, many of them even in a worse state than their poor countrymen at home. Were the case different, and those who emigrated from the island, capable of undertaking different branches of labour, both of a scientific as well as of a mechanical nature, there would be an increasing request for their services, as there would be more numerous situations which they would be able to fill.

Here perhaps it will not be out of place to mention the very bad system of training up tradesmen and artisans which exist at Malta; as this also, in connection with education, must have a very important bearing upon the interests of a nation. Here, a lad is put into a mechanic's shop by his parents, without any kind of agreement how long he is to continue at his business, or without any particular requisition from the master he is about to serve. It is commonly understood, that 'the boy is to learn the trade in the best way be can. There being no law on the subject, the apprentice is at liberty to leave the master just when he pleases, which often happens before he half knows his business, and then endeavours to set up for himself. Every one will see that such a plan is attended with many disadvantages, and calculated to repress improvement in the important branch of labour, of the mechanic. Such tradesmen, also, emigrating from the island, cannot be expected to meet with that good fortune which they would do were they perfectly trained in their different branches of labour. It is to be regretted that something like our apprentice system has not yet been adopted in Malta; it is certainly much needed, and could not fail to be productive of good.

Another cause for the poverty of the island lies in the entire want of a spirit of enterprise so relevant of the interests of the lower orders of society. Very few of those who possess property think of laying it out in some way so as to benefit their country; but choose rather to suffer it to lie by at a sordid interest, or to rust in their coffers.

It is worthy of remark, that the number of males in Malta is nearly equal to that of the females. (*) This destroys the false idea, generally received, that in warm climates more girls are born than boys; as it is also opposed to the state of the population in many of the northern and western countries of Europe. This would doubtless be the case universally, according to the analogy of nature, if various causes did not operate to destroy its course. The comparative little emigration which takes place in Malta, and the temperance of the male inhabitants contribute to mantain this regular law of our world.

" The Maltese are in general of an ordinary stature, strong, robust, of a brown complexion; one may easily recognise in their character the

---

(*) According to the last census, the number of males was 60,450 and that of females 63,040.

influence of the climate, and that mobility of sensation, gesture and features which characterize many people in the equinoxial regions of Africa. They are full of fire, and endowed with a penetrating imagination; they possess very lively passions, and are tenacious in their opinions, in their love and their hate. The action of a hot climate, beneath an almost continually serene sky, renders their physical and moral character very expressive; they do not know how to conceal their real sentiments with the mask of conveniency; in as much that there can be no where found men less disguised, and whose character can be more easily guessed by the physionomy. " D' Avalos tom. i p. 60, 61.

LANGUAGE AND EDUCATION.

Maltese language not derived from Phœnician—Attempts to reduce the Maltese to writing—Present system of National Education—Inconsistency of—Backwardness of the general mass of the people.

Notwithstanding the many attempts which have been made to refer the present Maltese dialect back to Phœnician original, by producing a few words and phrases which are corresponding in signification in both languages, the basis upon which the hypothesis is formed is too weak to sustain it against the abundant

proofs to the contrary. We shall not dwell
upon the almost necessary impossibility which
there exists against our coming to any solid
conclusion on the subject, from our inadequate
knowledge of the Punic tongue but shall draw
our inferences from the language itself as it
exists at the present day, which in its forms,
phrases, construction and idiom proves it to
be a dialect of the Arabic. We conceive that
if there are a few words which cannot now be
referred back to this source, this fact does not
destroy the abundant evidence which may be
brought forth in the whole body of the language. That there are such words we admit; but
that these have not become corrupted in their
etymology and pronunciation, cannot be proved any more than they can be shown to be a
part, or parts of the ancient Phœnician. The
vernacular Maltese comprehends the complete
Arabic alphabet, with the exception of some of
the dentals ; and the distinctive sound of the
gutturals has been preserved pure in many villages of the country, and in Gozo. In Valletta
this is not the case; several of the gutturals
have been dropped, and the whole dialect is
more corrupt, being mixed up with a greater
portion of foreign words, especially Italian.

Several attempts have been successively
made by different persons, within the last thirty
years, to reduce the Maltese dialect to writing ;
but these efforts having been chiefly the effect

of private exertion, without any support or
countenance from the government or the people, have all failed, whatever may have been
the comparative excellence of each plan adopted. This unsettled state of things, in regard
to language, has operated very much to the
prejudice of education among the people. All
instruction being communicated in the Italian,
the Maltese child cannot begin his studies on a
par with the children of other countries, because he must first learn a language entirely
different from his own, as a means of acquiring
the knowledge he seeks after. Under these
discouraging circumstances, it is no small proof
of the natural abilities of the Maltese, that
many of them have by their talents and acquire-
ments raised themselves to a distinguished
rank in literature and science. While this
state of things exists, however, there can be
little hopes of the mass of the people making
any very considerable progress in respect of
education. The mother tongue is so implanted
into their nature, that centuries must elapse, or
some great change take place in the common
order of things, before any attempt to eradi-
cate the language of the people can be successful.

Some small efforts were made to introduce
the Arabic as the chief medium of communi-
cating instruction in the government schools;
and if the ultimate object of this plan should

be energetically followed up, in a different
manner, there can be no doubt of its success.
To say nothing of the advantages which would
accrue to the Maltese should be put into possession of so extensive and useful a language
as the Arabic, it is the mother language of
their own, and consequently must be much
easier for their acquirement than any of the
western languages, which are entirely different
in their whole construction. The present plan
brought into use is briefly this : a new alphabet
has been formed for the Maltese dialect, consisting of Roman and several Arabic letters, in
which the children are to be instructed so as to
be capable of reading ; this then is to serve as
a medium of studying the Italian, the English,
and the Arabic ! This is not all, the language
used is such a compound of distorted Arabic
and Maltese terms and phrases, that it forms
quite a new dialect, which without considerable
instruction no Maltese can understand ! ! Who
will not at once see, that every attempt to in-
struct the generality of children, in so many
different and opposite tongues, must be rendered futile. It is preposterous, to think of
establishing any system for public education in
which the instruction is to be communicated
in no less than four languages. The time generally allowed for a child to remain at school
will not even suffice to acquire a tolerable
acquaintance with these ; and when is he to

make any progress in that useful knowledge which will make him a respectable and valuable member of society? If the Italian has obtained a partial footing in the town, it is an entire stranger in the country, and ought to be banished from the national system of education if it tends to increase the difficulties and inconveniences which exist without its addition. If by the present plan the Arabic is proposed to be the general language of the people, why are they encumbered with another, which will be of little use in such a case? And why teach the Maltese language? The dialect is already corrupt, and every effort to systemize it must be calculated to fix it more deeply in the minds of the children when on the contrary endeavours ought to be made at the onset for improving and bringing it up to the standard of that language which is to be made the general language of the country. To do this in Malta would not be attended with much more difficulty than in Syria, Egypt or Barbary, where the written language is the classical Arabic, but, the colloquial dialect, in many respects, not better than the Maltese. It is to be hoped that the present plan will be reformed before being carried to any considerable extent.

The above circumstances have had their influence in restraining the progress of education among the people, which, generally speaking, is at a low ebb. In many of the country villages, all the learning which exist is confined to the clergy, very few besides being able to read or write. In the town, besides the University and the Lyceum there is a Normal school for boys and girls, containing upwards of 500 children, and several others kept by private individuals and by religious communities. In the year 1836 by the zealous and praiseworthy efforts of Mrs. Austin, the lady of one of Her Majesty's Commissioners for Special Enquiry, four district schools were formed in the country, which have been completely successful. Later, Government having established male and female schools in all the principal villages and populous districts of Malta and Gozo, and new infant schools, public education has greatly extended. This is to be chiefly attributed to the indefatigable exertions and zeal of the present Director of Primary Schools the Rev. Dr. P. Pullicino. Considering the scanty means which the people enjoy of obtaining an education, we cannot wonder at their backward state, though we by no means intend to apply this remark universally; for, as we have said before, there are not a few among the Maltese who distinguish themselves by their literary attainments.

ZAPP-PLAYER

MUSIC, POETRY, AND SINGING.

Native musical instruments—Poetical composition—Songs —Maltese Proverbs, &c.

The Maltese are not very rich in native musical instruments ; and in their choice seem to have preffered with the inhabitants of Arabia, such as are more noisy than the softer instruments of the Arabs of northern Africa.   Even these, however, are getting into disuse, and their place is being supplied by companies of blind fiddlers who are almost in every village, and whose performances, if exhibited within the hearing of a man acquainted with the science, would certainly put him into a position to serve as an exact counterpart of Hogarth's *Enraged Musician*. The tamburine, a species of bag-pipe, the kettledrum, a hollow tube about half a foot in diameter with a distended skin over one surface, and a round stick tied to the centre of it, which is rubbed up and down with the hand, causing a most monotonous sound, (*) and several different shaped lyres, with from two to four strings,—form the native band of the Maltese country people. Of the above, the bagpipe or *zaqq*, as it is called, merits the most attention, as it is the most esteem-

(*) This instrument is called by the natives "rabbaba " or " zavzava. "

ed. This instrument is formed of an inflated dog skin, which is held under the left arm with the legs directed upwards, and having a mouth-piece by which the skin is filled and a flute or pipe played with both hands affixed to it. This instrument is generally accompanied by the tamburine and a dancing company, who move their bodies in graceful evolutions or ridiculous gestures to the sound of the duet. The accompanying sketch may convey some better idea of the rustic amusement.

It is in use amongst the lower classes, and almost exclusively during the last three days of Carnival.

However, the Maltese greatly participate in the musical taste of the Italians. There were at all times musical composers who distinguished themselves in Europe for their high merit in the Art. Azzopardi, Bugeja and Curmi obtained extensive fame by their compositions, and Nicolò Isouard is considered as the founder of Italian melody in France, where his name is historical.

The Maltese have the peculiar talent for poetry which is natural to all those nations who speak the Arabic language. The taste for this kind of composition has very much degenerated in the cities, but in the country it is met with in its original purity of style and expression. I have often stood and listened to individuals seated upon two opposite trees,

or engaged in some kind of labour, singing
answers to each other in rhyme, without any
previous meditation. This the natives call
takbeel. The subject vary according to circumstances, sometimes partaking of the nature
of epic poetry, and sometimes of satire upon
the faults or character of each. The tunes set
to these are in general somewhat wild, as is
the music of the Maltese in general, but a
wildness which is not without its romantic
beauty and harmony. In this respect, few will
fail to admire the singing of the natives as
they join in small companies, each taking a
part, which they maintain throughout the
whole performance.

Several native writers have lately subjected
this popular poetry to the established rules of
the Art, by the publication of lyric and epic
composition, which they have happily applied
both to satire and to novel-writing. The odes
by Professor Gio. Ant. Vassallo, Taylor's Psal-
ter and other essays are worthy of admiration
for their elegance and vigour. Turning the
poetic charms of the native tongue to religious
use, the Most Rev. Canon Mifsud Tommasi
composed a long series of sacred songs and
hymns, many of which are committed to memory by the humbler classes. These essays,
however, on the language of the country, are
not written with the intention of substituting
for Italian literature, which is the national li-

terature, the culture of a dialect systematically prohibited from all civil transactions, banished from the Courts of justice, from educational institutes, and, in the cities where education is of a higher grade, even from the pulpit. The poetry and literature of the Island has been and will always be the Italian, which is the written language of the Maltese. The native dialect properly appartains to the lower classes of the people.

I here subjoin two popular songs for the amusement of the reader, with a rough English translation, in order that he may judge somewhat of such amorous effusions.

SONG.

Hanina seyr insiefer,
  Ja hasra ma nichdoksh mighi,
Lilek, Alla yati es-sabar,
  U izommok flimhabba tighi.

Izommok fl' imhabba tighi,
  Biesh deyyem tiftakar fiyya,
Iftakar li yien habbeitek,
  Mindu kont chkeiken turbiyya.

Mindu kont chkeiken tarbiyya,
  Kalbi kollha ingibdet leik;—
Bl' ebda daul ma nista nimshi,
  Ghair biddaul ta sbih ghaineik,

Bid-daul ta sbíh ghaineik,
  Yien mesheit il passi tighi;
  Hanina seyr insiefer,
  Ja hasra ma niehdoksh mighi.

Meta niftakar li yiena seyyer,
  Dad-dulur sh'ygini kbir;
  K'Alla irid, o hanina!
  Ghad tgaudini u ingaudik.

Translation.

Beloved, I'm about to leave you
I sigh that I take you not with me,
May God give you now resignation,
And preserve you secure in my love.—

And preserve you secure in my love,
That you ever remember me;
Remember, I always have loved you;
Since the time I was but an infant.—

Since the time I was but an infant,
My heart has always been drawn after you
And I can walk in no other light,
But the light of your beautiful eyes.—

In the light of your beautiful eyes,
I have always directed my steps;
Beloved I'm going to leave you,
I sigh that I take you not with me.

How sore does the pain come upon me,
When I think I must soon depart;
But if Heaven be propitious, my dear,
We shall yet enjoy one another.

The following verses, which were furnished
me by a Maltese lady, I insert chiefly for the
sake of giving the reader an idea of the manner in which matrimonial alliances are entered
into by a portion of the town people. The four
persons introduced in the song are, the young
man, the *hottaba*, and the mother of the young
woman herself. In order to render the piece in-
telligible, it will be necessary to remise, that it
is not customary for a young man unacquaint-
ed with the lady with whom he has fallen in
love, to declare his passion in person, neither
would he be allowed to enter into her parents'
house; but he employs a third, generally an old
woman, who takes upon herself the office of endeavouring to bring about the match. This
character is called a *hottaba*, and is always
possessed with an exquisite gift for flattery;
a specimen of which will be readily noticed in
the song. I give a literal translation, in order
better to preserve the native idiom and phra-
seology.

SONG.

Tridu tafu shbeiba sh'taghmel,
  Min fil ghodu sa fil ghashia,
  Taghmel il bokli f'rasa,
  U tokghodlok fil gallaria.

Tokghodlok fil gallaria,
  Tibda taghmel in-namoor,
  Meta tara l'omma geja,
  Tibda tkofflok il maktur.

Il giuvni tiela u niezel,
  Halli yara hemsh shi shieha,
  Yibda tiela min fuk sisfel,
  Ghash mairidsh yibka bir-rieha.

Intaka ma nanna shiha,
  Kallha : mara tridsh takdini,
  Flusi ma nibzash ghalihom,
  Basta taghraf is-servini?

Sinyura donni nafek,
  Kont cheikuna tokghod hdeiya,
  Kem erfaitek, kem habbeitek,
  Kem ghazziztek geu'ideya.

Sinyura donni nafek,
  Yidirli ghandek ish-shbeibiet,
  Ghax kont ghaddeja mil hara ;
  Yidhirli raitha hdein il bieb.

Sinyura gheidli sh'ghandek,
  Kem narak malinconata.
  Ara'sh kalu fuk binti,
  Illi già binti namrata:

Iskot, Sinyura, iskot,
  Ilsna tan-nies tghid wisk shorti;
  Dika bintek tiflu taiba,
  Min yihoda ikollu shorti.

Inzel, binti, inzel,
  Hauna nanna trit tarak,
  Tinsab mara uisk antica,
  Li t'kliemha tik-konsolak.

Risposta yiena gitblek,
  Ohra fees yiena irrid,
  Baghatni il mahbub ta kalbek,
  Li bil piena yinsab marid.

Risposta inti gibtli,
  Ohra fees le ma natiksh;
  Dana il giuvni ommi tafu.
  B' zeugi niehdu ma tridnish.

Translation.

Intr. Would you know what a maiden does,
    From morning until evening?—
    She adorns her head with curls,
    And seats herself in the balcony.

She seats herself in the balcony,
And sets about making love;
When she sees her mother coming
She begins hemming her handkerchief.
The young man walks up and down,
To see if the old woman is there,
He traverses (the street) from one end
[to the other,
As he does not wish to remain with the
[smell (*).
He meets with an old grandmother,
And says; " woman will you help me,
I care nothing about money,
So as that you are able to serve me? "

*The bargain in struck, and the brokeress
goes to the house, of the young woman, and
meets with the mother.*

Hott. Madam, I think I know you.
When quite little you lived near me,
How oft I bore you, how much I lov'd you,
How oft I faundled you in my arms.
Madam, I think I know you,
I think you have several maidens,
For as I was passing through the streets,
I saw one standing at the door.
Madam, tell me what ails you,
For you appear very melancholy?

(*) A Maltese idiom for expressing failure in an undertaking.

Moth. Do you know what they say of my daugh-
     That she is already in love.   [ter,

Hott. Be easy, Madam, be easy,
     People's tongues say many things;
     Your daughter is a good girl,
     Whoever takes her will gain a fortune.

Moth. Come down, my daughter, come down,
     Here's grandmother desires to see you,
     She is a very old woman
     And with her words she will console you.
      The daughter descends, and the old wo-
man addresses her.

Hott. A message I have brought you,
     And wish one hastily in return,
     For the beloved of your heart has sent
     Who with pain is now quite ill.   [me,

Daugh. A message you have brought me,
     A hasty answer I will not give,
     For my mother knows this young man,
     And will not have him for my husband.

Besides the above, the Maltese have also a
large number of proverbs or adages in rhyme,
many of which preserve their strict Arabic original. These are still often used in conversa-
tion, but without any new additions, as the
taste for such composition has greatly degenerated since the introduction of the Italian lan-

guage.   The late Sig. Vassalli published a collection of these proverbs, some years ago, with
an Italian translation and explanatory notes,
which in the purity of their style and morals,
their figurative and enigmatical forms, contain
much of that good sense possed by the fore-
fathers of the Maltese. " The whole of these
adages, maxims, sentences, aphorisms and
phrases, which the natives have preserved from
time immemorable, by uninterrupted tradition,
form a species of national code, sanctioned
form time to time with the seal and authority
of the events or experiences of this or that pro-
verb, the truth of which is acknowledged as soon
as utterred. "

COSTUME.

Dress of the males—Dress of the females of the City—
Neatness of—Costume of the country-women.

In regard to the male population, the Maltese have in general adopted the Frank costume; but the native dress, which is still worn
to some extent by the lower class of people in
the town, is somewhat dissimilar, though very
peculiar. The chief difference is in the cap,
which resemble a long bag made of wool, hanging down behind, and dyed with various colors.
This article often forms a receptacle for mall

articles which the wearer wishes to carry about with him, and sometimes serves all the purposes of a purse. I observed the same kind of cap used among the Maronites of Mount Lebanon.

The girdle round the loins is still in use among the Maltese of the lower order; that made of cotton is called a *terha*, that of silk a *bushakka*. With this the pantaloons are confined round the waist, and is generally three or four yards in length. There can be no doubt that this is a relic of the oriental costume, introduced into Malta by the Arabs.

It is not common to see any in this dress with a jacket, its place being supplied by a *sedria*, or vest, which, in many cases, is ornamented down the front with several rows of round silver buttons, as large as a bird's egg. At other times, instead of these, the buttons consist of large pieces of money, especially quarter-dollar pieces and sometimes shillings or 6*d*. with long shanks fastened on to them. A Maltese cuts a very fine figure when he is thus set off, or is *in gala*, as they express it, with a long curl hanging down each side of his face, and having his fingers covered with many massy rings, of which they are particularly fond.

At the present day, the sandals are not used except by the country people; but there can be no doubt that they formed a part of the ancient native dress. These consist of two oblong pieces

of untanneld bull's hide, drawn round the foot
with two strings of the same material, and are
called *kork*. Some years ago, an old man used to
sit by the gate of Porta Reale, and it was worth
while seeing the dexterity with which he shod
the country people who applied to him. The
whole was done in a few minutes; for the customer first laid his foot on the extended hide,
and after taking the dimensions by just mark-
ing the circumference, the old man cut it off,
and making four holes in each piece for ears,
gave him a pair of strings, and all was over.

Many of the working classes in the country,
especially masons, wear over their shoulder
what they call a *horg*, in which they take their
provisions to town for the day, and carry it
home laden with the supplies for their family,
in the evening when their labour is over. It is
about three yards long and two feet wide, open
in the middle, so as to form a bag at each end.
The accompanying sketch will illustrate the
above description of the native dress of the
Maltese males.

It is observed however that during the last
few years especially, the national costume is
gradually growing into disuse, even with the
country people, and more particularly in those
villages near or in close contact with the town.

As to the costume of the ladies of the towns,
I fully accord with the observation of a Jesuit,
who passed through Malta in the latter end of

the last century. He says, "leur démarche et leur habillement sont si modestes, qu' on les prendroit par des religieuses." (*) I believe many, on their first arrival at the island, have had the same impression, that most of the females in Malta were nuns. It is rather to be regretted that so many have of late adopted the English costume, which is certainly far from being as simple, and by no means as modest and becoming. The bonnet, especially, as well as the gentleman's hat, are quite unnatural appendages; the one is satirically called an umbrella, and the other a kettle by many of the orientals (†).

The outer dress consists of a black silk petticoat, bound round the waist over a *body* of some other kind of silk or print; this is called a *half onnella*. The upper part is called the *onnella*, and is made of the same material with the former, drawn up into neat gathers for the length of a foot about the centre of one of the outer seams. In the seam of one of the remaining divisions is enclosed a thin piece of whalebone, which is drawn over the head, and forms an elegant arch, leaving the face and the neck

---

(*) Lettres Edifiantes et Curieuses. Tom. I. p. 315.

(†) As soon as the Frank costume was permitted to be worn in Damascus, the natives were quite surprised at the black hats, and so much were they shocked, at their unseemly shape and size, that they have ever since denominated an European as "Aboo Tanjara," the father of a pot.

perfectly open. The left arm is covered with
one part of this habit, and the right is used for
keeping down the angle of the other. The whole
is extremely neat; but it requires a peculiar
grace in walking to show it off to advantage.
In this respect the Maltese ladies are not defi-
cient, and here i beg to differ from Signor De
Avalos, who writes, "elles n'ont ni les gràces
des femmes Français, ni le maintien noble et
simple des Anglaises;" (*) unless he had written it concerning some of those who have adopted the English costume to which they have not
yet become much accustomed.

The dress of the country women does not
essentially differ in shape, but the material is
generally striped or barred native cotton, of a
very substantial quality. The head dress is
called a *tsholkana* instead of an *onnella*. The
doublett is in shape the same with the *half onnella*, but on particular occasions, such as a
marriage or a christening, they put on the
gezuira, which is a kind of petticoat of blue
cotton striped with white, drawn up in very
thick creases round the waist, and open on the
right side, where it is tied at different distances with bows of ribbon. The undermost habit
differs somewhat from that worn by the ladies
of the city, and is called a *dale*. This reaches
no farther down than the loins, upon which

(*) Tableau Historique de Malte. vol. I. p. 77.

another garment is tied round the waist, answering something to an under petticoat.

I have little doubt that the origin of the *onnella* must be sought for in the oriental veil. Laying aside the great probability that the latter was used in this island during the domination of the Arabs, I have been very much struck with the similiarity which there exist between both, when the *onnella* is made of some thin cloth, and suffered to hang down carlessly behind the back. Modern civilization and fashion, has, in my opinion, made this one barbarous appendage, one of the neatest head-dresses among the costumes of Europe.

The accompanying sketches will serve to illustrate the above description.

AMUSEMENTS.

Procession: Good Friday—Easter Sunday—Festival of St. Gregory—Curious article in marriage contracts—Feast of St. Paul—Races—Carnival—Parata—Origin of—Giostra or Slippery pole—Boat race.

The principal recreation of the Maltese have in general, some connection with their religious ceremonies. The numerous processions, which however of late have been very much diminished, afford opportunities to the stranger of seeing every rank and class of the peo-

ple, in their best attire, congregated together
in crowds to witness the scene. The two chief
occasions when these ceremonies are of opposite natures; one being that of Good Friday,
intended to celebrate the death and passion of
our Saviour, and the other the procession of
St. Gregory, which is continued until the present day in commemoration of some signal public deliverance. The former takes place in the
town on Holy Thursday. The train leaves the
church of *ta Giesu* a little before sunset, the
fratelli and friars walking in file on each side
of the street, with huge lighted wax tapers in
their hands, and chanting as they follow the
statues, which are carried before them at equal
distances in the processions. These images are
in general of a large size, and represent the
various sufferings of the Saviour until he is
laid in the sepulchre; which last is a splendid
canopy, with rich curtains tassellated with gold
having a figure as large as life stretched beneath them. After traversing several of the
streets, the procession reenters the church from
which it came out.

Very early on Easter Sunday, before day-
light, a great crowd with lamps in their hands
assemble around the door of the Greek catholic
church, from whence they take a large image,
representing the resurrection of our Lord, with
a flag in his hand. With this they proceed
through Strada Reale, amidst the joyful accla-

mations of the people who follow it, upon their arrival at the small church of the Vittoria, a gun is fired from the cavalier, which is a signal for a general run as far as the walls of the city. After traversing several other streets, they deposit the image in the same church from which they took it. I would observe, that this procession is unattended by any of the clergy, excepting the Greek Catholic Priest.

The feast of St. Gregory consists of a procession composed of the *fratelli* (*) of all the churches, the clergy of all the different parishes of the towns and villages, the canons of the cathedral, and the Bishop, who assemble together at the village called Casal Nuovo, and walk as far as Zeitun, the whole company joining in the responses of the Great Litany, which is

(*) In order that the reader may understand what is meant by this term, I would just observe, that connected with almost every church is a fraternity consisting of laymen, who join themselves together by contributing a certain sum yearly into a common fund, which is generally laid out upon the church, or otherwise disposed of by them for religious purposes. Each fraternity has a president, and meets often in order to talk over the affairs connected with their body, which generally turns upon decorating the church, or their own particular altar, the ordering of illuminations, processions, &c. Each fraternity wears a particular uniform corresponding with their banner, which is generally borne before them when they walk in procession.

The fratelli of the convent of St. Domenico, under the patronage of the MADONNA DEL ROSARIO, consist entirely of persons who have some relation with the law faculty such as advocates, notaries, &c.

pronounced by the chief priest of each order. On their arrival at Zeitun, they all visit the old church of St. Gregory, where at a particular part of the ceremony, the whole crowd exclaim three times, " Misericordia. " Afterwards, some of the people spend the remaining part of the day in eating and drinking and various kinds of amusements. The origin of this feast is involved in obscurity; but it is commonly supposed to be founded upon a general vow of the inhabitants, on their deliverance from a great plague; some say, a large swarm of locusts which once devasted the island.

It was a common occurrence for country females to stipulate with their intended husbands that they should take them once a year to see the principal feasts of the island. St. Gregorio is one of the above; and the bridegroom made it a point, if possible, to become the standard - bearer in the processions of the lay brethren of his village. This was considered a great honor, and consequently the privilege was held out to the highest bidder. The individual who succeeded in obtaining the prize, agreed with his bride, that he would meet her at the village where the procession terminates.

Among the many ludicrous songs and compositions used on the days of carnival the following is not uncommon, and as it alludes to the custom I have just mentioned, I shall transcribe it with an English translation.

G

L'AGHRAYES YAGHMLU IL PATTIYIET.

Fl' iscritta matrimoniali
Yaghmlu il pattiet conjugali.
Li yiehoda fil festi principali.
Yonsobha fuk il hait,
Yishtreelha shriek cubbait,
Li ikun tal cannebusa
Ghash minnu tiggosta is-sinyura gharusa.

Translation.

THE SWEETHEARTS' BARGAIN.

In the wedding contract
They make conjugal agreements;
That he (the bridegroom) shall take her to prin-
cipal feasts.
Shall set her upon the wall
Shall buy her a slice of sweetmeat,
Made up of hempseed,
For that's the kind which the bride likes best.

Besides the above, there are several other
processions which take place in the town, the
principal of which are those of St. John and
St. Paul. On these occasions, the exterior of
the church dedicated to the saint is illuminated
with numerous lamps, and bonfires are lighted
up in several of the streets. The feast of St.
Peter and St. Paul, called by the natives
L' Imnaria, celebrated at the Old City, is another principal occasion of amusement. After

the services of the church, crowds proceed to the Boschetto about two miles distant, and dividing into companies, spread themselves with the refreshments they bring with them, while many of the country people amuse themselves in dancing and singing, and many other rural gratifications. Just below the city, on this day, there is also a race of horses, mules and asses, which are entirely unharnessed, and the riders without and means of maintaining their position except their legs, which they fix under the animal's belly, while with a thong in each hand they belabour the poor beasts until they reach the goal. Another race of this kind on the feast of St. Rocco, is held at the Pietà, outside the gates of Porte des Bombes, which was instituted after the Islands were freed from the plague in the year 1693. The prizes at these races consist of large flags of various coloured silk, which the winners generally carry about the streets the next day, together with their animals covered with garlands of flowers and ribbons.

The Carnival is another source of popular amusement; this begins on the sunday preceding Lent, and lasts for three days. The afternoon is the principal time of the feast, during which numerous persons in masks are seen walking about the streets, endeavouring to amuse themselves, and to be a source of amusement to others. The variety of dresses used on these occasions is beyond description. Not a few pride themselves in playing all kinds of antics in a black habit, with long red horns, and a huge tail of the same colour. Coaches filled with ladies follow in a train through the principal streets, who readily engage in pelting confits and peas with any of the bystanders who will enter the lists with them. The number of respectable persons, however, who mask in the public streets has greatly diminished within the last few years and it is to be hoped, that their good example will soon be followed by an entire relinquishment of so absurd and foolish a diversion. Though on the other hand it is to be observed, that there are very few countries so void of amusement for the lower classes, like Malta. This is one of the principal reasons why it would be difficult to suppress entirely these Carnival follies. An attempt on the part of the government to suppress the first day of Carnival (Sunday) in 1846 was attended with serious disturbances in fact by a popular tumult, and was the cause of the recall of the then Governor Sir Patrick Stuart. The first Sunday after the Carnival, most of those persons who have masked repair to the parish church of Casal Zabbar, called *della Grazia*, by way of penance for their follies.

On saturday preceding the first day of the feast, the *Parata* is celebrated. This consists of several companies of men dressed up in gay ribbons, and armed with wooden staves and shields, who meet together under the houses of the wealthy, and perform several evolutions, striking their shields and dancing at the sound of music. This is concluded by raising up a little girl, splendidly arrayed, and girded with a small dagger, which is taught to wave while the band plays the national anthem, "God save the Queen." In time of the Order, they proceeded to the palace to receive permission for the celebration of the Carnival. Their request was signified to the Grandmaster by one of the knights, and upon the boon being granted, they immediately performed a dance in front of the palace, and afterwards before the door of any other person, whom they thought would pay them for their trouble.

The origin of this amusement must be sought for in the annals of pagan rites, which christianity has not succeeded in abolishing in several countries of Europe. In a work on Malta "Par un voyageur Francais," the author ranks it with a popular feast very ancient in Thessaly, the *Salzea* of the Babylonians, the *Chronia* of the Athenians, and the *Saturnalia* of Rome, which many of the early christians continued, notwithstanding the zealous efforts which were made by the church to abolish them.

Another very famous diversion of the Maltese is the *Giostra*, which takes place on the anniversary of the victory gained over the

Turks, when they made their attack upon the island, in the reign of La Valette. This sport is accompanied with races of boats which run part of the length of the harbour, the prizes being awarded by the Government. The *Giostra* is a large barge, anchored in an open place in the centre of the port, having a long tapering pole placed horizontally from the head, with a small flag fixed on at the end, and made very slippery with grease, soap and several other ingredients. At a given signal, a number of naked boys are ready mounted on the barge, who immediately begin the task of endeavouring to seize the flag. One after another they continue tumbling into the water, and raising again to renew the attempt. Gradually the greasy matter begins to diminish, and they are able to advance farther; but an hour generally elapses before the prize is seized, and very seldom before some accident has happened among the competitors, many of whom strike their limbs on the pole in their fall into the water. This amusement generally attracts a numerous quantity of boats round the barge filled with hundreds of spectators both male and female.

ADMINISTRATION OF JUSTICE.

Origin of the present Maltese code—Confusion of—Enumeration of the Courts—Suppression of the Bishop's Tribunal—Trial by Jury introduced—Commission to draw up new codes—Result of their labours—Language in which the Maltese codes ought to be written.

The Order of St. John of Jerusalem made over to the Maltese a deposit of written and consuetudinary laws, copied from the ancient Roman and Ecclesiastical legislations. At that period, Sicily followed the same course; for, since that island had come under the dominion of the Spaniards, it was subject to the power of the Vatican, which thought itself capable of regulating the morals of whole nations, with the confusion of laws one thousand two hundred years old,—a confusion increasingly aggravated by the *Bullarium*, the mass of the Pope's Decretals and those of the *Stravaganti*. It appears therefore, that the legislation of Malta was the same with that of Sicily. In later times, it is true, this island enjoyed several laws of her own, such as those of Manoel de Vilhena, Rohan, and other Grandmasters, who from time to time issued proclamations or provisionary regulations for particular cases; yet, both the Municipal Constitutions, as well as the above Proclamations, were, for the most part, very badly disposed, for behind the times and the people which they governed, and coined, without exception, upon the impress of the above mentioned constitutions.

As to the Judiciary proceedings of the country they were based upon the *Rito Siculo;* and the organization of the courts conformed to the same.

It cannot fail to surprise, that the same disorders and even greater than those which existed in the legislation, during the reign of the Order, continued to exist in the island, in vigour up to a certain period, under British rule. Half a century ago, this confusion of laws was not very sensibly felt by an enduring and docile people like the Maltese. The subjects of a theocracy, they found a remedy for their real evils in the religious sentiments which supported them. The case, however, is now different ; and is not from the reflection of the light of European civilization, which shines upon them in the centre of the Mediterranean, under the auspices of Great Britain,—the Maltese people, although the same in many respects, have still become capable of valuing their own true state, as also the state of their legislations.

The code of the Grandmaster Rohan is in full force up to the present moment in several principal dispositions. Very few of the salutary laws, however, therein contained (such, for example, as those which have reference to fathers of families and vagabonds,) are followed out ;

while a multitude of such as are incoherent, or written *ad terrorem*, or incompatible with the judiciary order newly introduced, or repugnant with the newly established rule of commercial jurisprudence, (which require laws corresponding more or less between the countries which have commercial intercourse with each other) are in actual vigour.

Where provision is not made in this code, (which very frequently happens) the indigested farrago of *Corpus Juris* of Justinian is brought in to supply the want. This monstruous collection of the monument of knowledge, barbarity, and imbecility of various Roman legislators, (as it is called by Filangieri) is much less adapted for Malta, than for any other country, subject as it is to the dominion of England. A country like Malta, which draws its chief resources from commerce, and under the rule of the most commercial people in the world, should not be governed by the code of a people anti-commercial by nature, and by political disposition. The formulæ, the solemnities, and the actions of law are so many insopportable shackles to commerce and good faith, and the expedition necessary in all commercial transactions.

The infinite number of writers on the Roman Law, Disertationists, Commentators, Casuists, Deciders, the Italian *Rote*, and more especially the *Rota Romana* all come in to the aid of the already mentioned compilations, whenever doubts, anomalies, contradictions, either in the letter or the spirit of the laws occur, which is almost always the case. But it scarcely ever happens that, in recurring to this host of writers, one ever succeeds in arriving at a clearer understanding of the case; for they are even more confused and contradictory among themselves than the law itself. Notwithstanding all this, the authority of each is admitted in our tribunals, without any distinction; so that writers for other countries, for other times, under governments entirely different from that under which this island at present exists, are very often the legal criterion by which the magistrate pronounces his decision.

To the above mentioned sources of the native Legislation, there must be added the immense mass of Proclamations and Notifications which the Governors of the island have incessantly published; very often contradictory to each other, and almost continually revoking or amending the preceding. These at present form seven folio volumes.

In 1814 Sir Thomas Maitland made an attempt to reform the procedures, and to organize the Courts of Justice on a new plan. To this end he published a general constitution for all the courts, and a statute for each one in particular, which are undoubtedly to be commended for their simplicity and perspicuity; nevertheless we cannot refrain stating, from practical observation on this partial reform, that the principal design of the legislator was only to burden the public with a tax, whenever they had a case to bring before the court, or had occasion to claim their own property. Even at present, the weight of the expenses of the several courts, differing from that of the Registrars through every Hall, is indescribable; and this, besides what is necessary for the pay of advocates, legal procurators, &c. In fact, in many cases, it is only left in power of the rich to obtain justice in the tribunals of Malta. However in the year 1814 the organization of tribunals underwent several alterations: and the reforms, which had taken place in these last years, were intended to lessen the number of tribunals, in order to come to a simpler and easier administration of justice.

The Following is a list of the tribunals :
First Hall of the Civil Court.
Second Hall of Civil Court.
Criminal Court.
First and Second Halls of Appeal.
Criminal Court of the Police Magistrates.
Civil Court of ditto.
District Court of the Syndics in the villages.
Deputation for Marriage lagacies.

All this without mentioning the appeal to London, or enumerating the different courts in the island of Gozo.

The suppression of the Bishop's Court, which

took place in 1828, cannot be mentioned but with praise; its jurisdiction is at present confined to cases entirely spiritual. The abuses of this tribunal had become insupportable, and the appeals made therefrom to the Court of Rome were not only attended with heavy expenses, but were also interminable.

Trial by Jury in certain determinable criminal cases, where condemnation for life to the public works, or sentence of death is the penalty to be inflicted, was introduced by virtue of a Proclamation issued in the year 1829. This was the first political concession granted to the Maltese by the British Crown, after twenty nine years of its dominion over these Islands; and the Maltese people looked at this concession as a pledge of the determined intention of H. M's Government, to make them partakers of every benefit that belongs to all British subjects. Concedering this procedure both in a purely judiciary point of view, as well as morally and politically in its relation with the actual state of the civilization of the people, we may venture to say, that its advantage is of an unquestionable and undeniable great benefit. The Jury, as it is framed after the French system, and in the manner in which it is conducted here, has received a satisfactory and sudden development in a short process of years: and so far as experience shows, the good sense, the impartiality and religion of the Maltese Jurors were without exception highly commended. Such good success, obtained from the legislative measure and education of the people, convinced the Government to extend, in the year 1844, this procedure for all crimes punishable with imprisonment for five or more years, and in the year 1855 by the promulgation of the New Code of Criminal Procedure for all crimes without distinction, comprising also abuse of the liberty of the Press.

All the inconveniences above referred to in the general system of the legislation of Malta, in the organization of the Courts, and in the judiciary order, have induced the inhabitants to demand a reform from Great Britain, several times within the last few years. Their reasonable request was at length attended to, and a Commission was formed in order to draw up a new code of laws, after the model of those most recently enacted in Europe. For the accomplishment of this purpose, the persons first elected were J. Stoddart, Chief Justice of the island, J. Kirkpatrick, Esq. Robert Langslow, Esq., Attorney General at Malta, with Dr. V. C. Bonnici, and Dr. J. G. Bonavita, two of Her Majesty's native judges.

Several months after the emanation of the above commission the question arose. "Whether the English or the Italian was to be the text in which the new laws for Malta ought to be written." The English members, with the

exception of John Kirkpatrick Esq. held out for
the English language, and the Maltese for the
Italian. The arguments on both sides were
examined by the Colonial Department, and the
Italian was approved. The matter finally terminated in the revocation of the Commission,
and the appointment of another in the persons of five Maltese members. Up to the year
1835, the result of their labours was the *Penal
Code*, and the *Laws of Procedure and Penal
Organization*, which are now put into practice.
To these we must refer, rather than to any
other source in order to decide upon the fitness
or unfitness of the persons deputed for the
accomplishment of the desired end. The chief
basis of the design, as is believed, was laid by
Dr. J. G. Bonavita, the principal advocate for
the Italian language to be used in writing out
the Maltese legislation.

These two projects of new Codes of laws
were published in virtue of a public notice
issued on the 21st July 1830, in which a general invitation was given for an experimental
sanction within a fixed period. Consequently
some of the lawyers and people applied to the
Secretary of State for obtaining a longer time.
he referred the application to the consideration
of the late Commissioners of Inquiry, who
complied with their demand. At last, in the
year 1837 the compilation was suspended, till
a report on the same be obtained from the said

Commissioners of Inquiry; and therefore the experimental sanction had no effect. It appears however, that these projects of laws possess some of the features and qualities of a good body of laws, viz. integrity, method and perspicuity, yet the Maltese people did not give them a welcome reception from the moment of their pubblication; and notwithstanding the clamours, which were raised against them especially by the legal faculty, the general invitation given for any observation or suggestion to be made concerning them, within a limited period, passed away without any criticism having been presented. It is melancholy to say, that these projects of laws were rather opposed with a view to destroy them than to reform their organization, whilst they were susceptible of having a reform. In the year 1839, after the recommendation of the Commissioners of Inquiry, the Government appointed the president of the Court of Appeal, Sir J. G. Bonavita, LL. D. and the Judge Dr. Chappell to revise and amend the original project in order to put it to a trial for three or five years. The amended project was, in the year 1842, submitted to Government, and afterwards it was committed to Mr. Andrews Jameson, a learned Scoth lawyer, to examine its state, and to bring it into harmony with the spirit of the English law. Dr. Jameson made his report in the year 1843, and in the following year the local Go-

vernment appointed a Commission consisting
of two Maltese compilers, to whom the report
was communicated for making their observations and suggestions. This Commission did
not approve Mr. Jameson's views, suggestions
and principal alterations ; and in spite of that
disapprobation, the Code was, for the last time
revised by the Crown advocate, and in virtue
of a notice issued in the year 1848, was exposed
to the public criticism. Lately in the year 1850,
the same was examined and discussed in the
first session of the new Council of Government.
The various alterations and suggestions made by
the Scotch lawyer, are highly commendable,
especially with reference to the Criminal procedure ; but on account of the different persons
engaged to revise and reorganize the project,
it is most certain that it does not offer that
order, regular structure, harmony of principles,
and uniformity of spirit, which influenced the
members of the first Commission in framing its
original construction.

With regard to the language in which the
laws for Malta are to be written, the decision
of H. M's Government is very plausible. Indeed, it is a principle not only of justice, but
also of interest for the Maltese people to follow
up that, which the good sense, legal reasoning,
ideas and habits of this population, can sug-
gest. From a very long course of years,
the Italian language, is the language of the

Maltese legislation of the Court of Justice, of business and commercial transaction, (if we except the remotest time, when only the Latin language was also promiscuously used); and although the language, of the various nations, who in subsequent times ruled over Malta was totally stranger to our Country, yet they always respected the principle of the Italian language, as legal at Malta; and also distinguished all that, which now and then under a false point of view concerns the ruling nation, from that, which in reality promotes the interest, and lessens the wants of the ruled people. Abiding by this fact, and considering the *present* state of language at Malta, the extensive knowledge of the Italian to every class, as the only *written* language of the country, and the very limited number of such persons as can read and write, who have any acquaintance of the English, it appears rather strange, that one would think of giving a Code of laws written in a language entirely unknown and foreign to the people of Malta !

The opinion of the English members of the above mentioned Commissiom perhaps aimed at the difficulty of establishing the Italian here as the language of the laws ; whilst through the help of decided efforts, the Government, might arrive at a future time to extend the knowledge of the English in such a manner as to establish it as the last language of the

Country. But we think, that it is impossible to effect in this Island such a change, which though in a very limited population, could not take place either in any period, or among any other people. The efforts made by the Government to extend as much as possible the knowledge of the English language among all classes of society of the Maltese are very praisworthy, as they would tend to diffuse knowledge, and blend intimately our interest and political relation with Great Britain; but to effect such an end at the expense of the Italian seems impossible. The Italian, has become the written language of the Island, not by chance, or election; but it is the result of permanent circumstances, which existed and will exist for ever. The geographical position, the various relations with neighbouring countries, and the great extent of trade with the Mediterranean coast, where the Italian is exclusively the language of commercial transaction, are conditions, which caused that language to exist and survive at Malta for many centuries, amidst foreign dominions, which probably have had the same interest, that Great Britain has to substitute its own tongue. Our Home Government, having the inclination to improve the welfare of the Maltese, ought to have the interest and to protect the diffusion of the Italian among the people as far as its own language; but both the English and Italian do not find the same disposition of mind to acquire them; and the same conflict, which at present exists, will always exist between them as the former is only useful to some of the people, and the latter is indispensably written and cultivated by the most enlightened portion of the inhabitants, who do not deem it their interest to acquire the English. Therefore, whatever may be the attempts intended to be carried on to put an end to the existence of the Italian language, in which our laws are written; and whatever are the measures to be taken to extend the knowledge of the English, they not only never arrive to settle the object in view, but also they will leave the dispute, which of the two languages shall have the preeminence. The English cannot be expected to gain an ascendency over the Italian, even after the laps of centuries ; and therefore if any definite plan be otherwise pursued to effect a change in the language of the people, it will be detrimental to the interest of the British Government, as also to the interests of the Maltese.

The reform in the Maltese Legislation, has made rapid progress of late years, which has been attended with success.—The new Codes of Criminal Procedure, Police Regulations, and Commercial Laws are already in force, and many substantial parts of the Civil Laws have undergone a change in conformity with the system adopted by the most civilized states of Europe.

PART THIRD

ITINERARY OF THE

ISLAND OF MALTA.

PART THIRD.

DIVISION OF THE ISLAND.

THE Island of Malta may be said to contain two principal cities, three towns, and twenty-two *casals* or villages scattered over a part of the latter from their size, population and building might be termed towns; and a few have been dignified with that title by several of the Grandmasters. As, for instance, Casal Zebbug is sometimes called Città Rohan; Casal Curmi, Città Pinto; and Casal Zabbar, Città Hompesh.

The two principal cities are Valletta and Città Notabile; the latter is called also Città Vecchia, or in Maltese Mdina, and situate about the centre of the island. Borgo or Vittoriosa, Senglea and Burmula or Cospicua, the three chief towns, occupy the two promontories on the opposite side of the harbour, towards the east of Valletta.

In order to render the different descriptions as clear as possible, I shall class those objects which are most interesting and deserving of notice under separate heads, though by so

doing, I may sometimes be found guilty of reception. Valletta being the capital, I shall
commence with it; including its suburbs and
fortifications.

DETAILS OF THE CITY OF VALLETTA.

Foundation of the city—Its situation—Streets—Houses—
Mole—Warehouses on—Health Office—Exterior fortifications
—Gates.

Valletta is situated on the east side of the
island, in Long. 14º 30' 25" E. Lat. 35º 53'
4" N. It is built upon a promontory of land
anciently called Shaab-er-Ras, *the jutting out
of the cape.* Before the arrival of the Order,
the capital of the island was the Città Notabile; and the present site of Valletta was occupied by a few huts, and defended by the fort
of St. Elmo, which at that time was very in-
significant compared with its present size and
strength. The first stone of the new city was
laid by the Grandmaster La Vallette, on the
28th of March 1566; and the whole was completed by his successor Pietro del Monte, on
the 15th of May 1571.

The situation of Valletta is very convenient
for commerce; the appearance of the town from
the sea is delightful, nor does the interior produce the disappointment so common in towns
of the south of Europe.

The streets are regular and were formerly paved with hard stone; they are now macadamized, a most inconvenient system which greatly lessens the well-known cleanliness of the towns of Malta. The streets are dusty in summer and muddy in winter; and the mud resulting therefrom is carried into the harbours by the heavy rains. At night-time they are lighted with gas, which was introduced in 1857 and lately extended to the three towns on the other side of the Grand Harbour.

From the declivity on which some part of the city is built, many of them are steep, with side-walks composed of stairs, which the author of the piece entitled *Farewell to Malta*, erroneously attributed to Lord Byron, recollected with no very pleasent associations, if we may judge from the line " Adieu ye caused streets of stairs." The town is kept remarkably clean, being swept every morning.

The houses are all built of stone, and very generally comprise three stories. Besides the windows opening into the street and yard, each dwelling has one or two balconies jutting out several feet from the wall and varying from six to twenty in length. These awkward protuberances are sometimes open, and sometimes covered on the top; and are supplied with glass windows which can be opened or shut at pleasure. However much of these serve to destroy the beauty of the external appearances of the

H

buildings, they are very comfortable retreats for the inmates, both in summer and winter as from them they can espy all that transpires in the street without being exposed to the effects of either.

The houses have all flat-roofed terraces, which serve the double purpose of being an agreeable resort for a walk, and receptacle for the rain which falls during the winter; from whence it runs into the cistern, with which almost every dwelling is provided. In case rain should fail, water can be let into the cisterns through underground canals which communicate with the acqueduct. Such houses as do not possess this convenience are supplied by the public fountains, of which there are several in different parts of the city.

On the mole of the Grand Harbour, near the Custom-house, on a somewhat raised platform, is a circular fountain, in the centre of which was a fine bronze statue of Neptune, holding the trident in one hand and the escutcheon of the Grandmaster Alofio Wignacourt, by whom it was raised, in the other. This piece of art is the work of Giovanni Bologna, a pupil of Michaelangelo.

This statue was removed to the Courtyard of the Palace of the Grandmaster by Governor Sir Gaspard Le Marchant.

The semi-circular row of rooms situate round this fountain was built by the Grandmaster

Raymond Despuig, and intended as a fish-market; for which purpose it is at present used.

The long excavated passage, leading from this division of the mole to that beyond the custom-house, was cut by the Grandmaster John P. Lascaris, and called after his name Lascaris Gate. Over these was a fine house and garden attached, built by the Grandmaster Lascaris, for the enjoyment of the knights during the summer months.—This building has however lately been demolished and a fortress has been constructed in the defence of the harbour. The parterre which leads into the dwelling, formed by the terraces of the storehouses beneath, is very spacious, and forms a delightful walk with a good view of the harbour.

The long range of warehouses beyond the custom-house, as far as the Calcara Gate, was also work of Lascaris. Those just below the Calcara Gate were erected by the Grandmaster Zondadari. Further up still are nineteen other magazines, each two stories high, and very spacious. These were built by Emmanuel Pinto, and intended for merchantile stores. In the centre of the range is a bronze bust of the founder with a Latin inscription,

PUBLICÆ COMMODITATIS META.

At present these are used as Ordnance stores. The mole was begun by Zondadari, and completed during the reign of Manoel de Vilhena A. D. 1726.

The fortifications which surround the town are very high, and many of them formed partly of the native rock; the walls measure about fifteen feet wide, and are composed chiefly of the common limestone of the country. Their whole circumference is two miles and a half. The ditch which croses the peninsula from the Quarantine to the Great harbour, cutting off all communication with the city, is about 1000 feet in length, 120 feet deep, and as many wide: this is crossed by five bridges: one before the principal gate, called Porta Reale, and the others connected with the covered ways leading from St. James's and St. John's cavalier. These two fortresses flank the chief entrance into the town and command the whole country before, and the city in the rear. One is at present unoccupied; St. James's to the left contains a detachment of the British garrison. Each is capable of quartering five hundred men.

Beyound the counterscarp are many outworks and glacis built in the same massy style, and well supplied with cannon, rendering the city one of the best defencible in the world. One would imagine that all these fortifications must require a great force to man them properly; yet, it was calculated by the Cavalier Foulard, that 12,000 troops would suffice for the defence of the port, and the security of the walls. During the existence of the Order, the knights of each Language had a particular post assigned to them in case of an attack. The division was as follows: to the knights of Provence, the Rampart of St. John, with its cavalier.

Auvergne,———St Michael.

France, ———St. James, with its cavalier.

Italy, ———St. Peter and Paul.

Arragon, ———St. Andrew.

England, Platform of St. Lazarus.

Germany, Rampart of St. Sebastian.

Castille, ———Sta. Rarbara.

The city is closed by three gates:

Porta Reale, which is the chief entrance from the country, and which was recently widened, is divided into two passages for the convenience of the public.

Porta Marsamuscetto from the Quarantine harbour, and the *Marina Gate* from the Great harbour. Besides the above, there are two sally ports: one leading from the outer walls of fort St. Elmo, and the other before the rampart of St. Lazarus, which is at present open for the convenience of those who live on the opposite side of the quarantine harbour. Here they can take boats and cross over as far as Sliema or fort Tignè until sunset, when it is closed for the night. This passage is called the Jews' Sally Port.

The principal street of the city is Strada Reale, which extends from the gate of the same name, as far as the castle of St. Elmo; a distance of three quarters of a mile. The chief streets which run parallel with this are:

Strada Forni	Strada Stretta.
—Mercanti	—Zecca
—St. Paolo	—St. Ursola.

The principal cross-streets are:

Strada Mezzodì	Strada Vescovo.
—Britannica	—San Cristoforo.
—St. Giovanni	—San Domenico.
—St. Lucia	—Teatro.

Strada San Nicola.

We shall commence our details by describing

THE CASTLE OF ST. ELMO.

This fortress is built on the extremity of the peninsula of land which separates the two chief harbours of the island. The present site of St. Elmo was anciently called *della Guardia;* as here a watch was constantly kept to notice the entrance of all vessels into both harbours. Here also was a small chapel dedicated to St. Erasmus or St. Elmo, the tutelar saint of seamen; from which the fort derives its name. The fort was first erected by order of the viceroy of Sicily, on the occasion of an attak of the Turks in 1438. When the knights of Rhodes took possession of Malta, they soon saw the importance of having this point well fortified, and after an invasion of the Turks, when it was first projected to build a new city on Mount Shaaber-Ras, by order of the Grandmaster Jean D'

Omedes; in the year 1552, this fortress was much enlarged, and destined to form the citadel of the town. The work was carried on and completed under the direction of the Grand Prior of Capua; masons and other workmen were brought over from Sicily for the purpose.

In 1565, the eighth year of the reign of La Vallette, Solyman, enraged at the seizure of a Turkish gallion belonging to the chief black eunuch of his seraglio, vowed the destruction of Malta; and for that purpose, destined a formidable armament under Dragut, the admiral of the Algerine fleet, which appeared off the island in the Month of May. The first point of attack determined on by Solyman's general was at St. Elmo, which was usually garrisoned by sixty men, under the command of one knight, but such was the importance of the place, that it was thought expedient to add a reinforcement. Accordingly sixty knights and a company of Spanish infantry were sent to support it.

On the 25th of the same month the Turkish artillery began to batter the fort both from the sea and land. In few days a breach was effected and a most bloody contest ensued, which must soon have ended in the entire destruction of so small a garrison, had no fresh supplies of troops continually arrived during the night, from Borgo, in boats, which took back the wounded from the fort. The ravelin was next stormed by the besiegers, and fell into their hands after a loss on their part of about 3000 men; but insensible to this loss, they continued the attack with unexampled ardour. In the mean time the courage of the garrison was unabated, but seeing that the ravelin was taken, the fort exposed, the greater part of the artillery dismounted, the ramparts in ruins, with but very few soldiers to defend them, they deputed a knight to wait upon the Grandmaster to request that they might evacuate the fort. La Vallette, though secretly deploring the fate of so many brave men who had fallen, yet, knowing the importance of the place, would not consent to its abandonment on the most urgent entreaties from many of the Order. By a stratagem which he formed, he raised the emulation and jealousy of the petitioners, who were now determined to die rather than yield up their posts. On the 16th of June, a general assault was made by the enemy, and the walls were laid even with the rock on which they were built. The Turks now entered the pitch where a fierce engagement took place; or while a continual fire was kept up from both sides, the parties grappled with each other after they had broken their pikes in the contest. The assault continued for six hours, when the enemy began to give way, and sounded a retreat after having lost 3000 men. Seventeen knights perished in the breach, and 300 soldiers were either killed or wounded.

A reinforcement of 150 men from Borgo who voluntarily offered themselves for the service, was now sent over to the fort; but this was the last time such assistance could be afforded. The Turkish commander managed to land a force on the opposite side of the Renella creek, which hindered any boat from crossing over to the help of the besieged. On the 21st. three assaults were made, and were as often repulsed, until night put a stop to the contest.

On the following day the assault was renewed by day-break, and after defending the breach for four hours, only sixty men remained to man it. At 11 o'clock, the Janissaries made themselves masters of the Cavalier, and the Turkish commander entered the fort. Not one knight was left alive and few remaining soldiers perished in the breach. The loss of the enemy is estimated at 8000, while the Order lost 300 knights and about 1300 soldiers. The inhuman Turk, wishing to revenge the death of his troop, ordered a search to be made among the dead and wounded for the knights whose hearts he had ripped out and often cutting their breasts in the shape of a cross, commanded them to be set afloat on boards, designing that the tide should carry them over to St. Angelo towards Borgo. By way of reprisal La Valette ordered all the prisoners to be put to death, and loading his cannon with their still bleeding heads, fired them into the enemy's camp.

In the following year, after the reimbark-
ment and defeat of the Turkish expedition,
when the first stone of the city of Valetta was
laid, the fort of St. Elmo was repaired and fortified, and built in a more regular form than it
was before. In the year 1687, under the Grandmaster Carafa, the fortress was almost rebuilt,
and in the commencement of the eighteenth
century the surrounding bastions were added
by the Grandmaster Raimondo de Perellos
y-Roccaful. The bastions, as also the fort, are
built of a very hard limestone, called by the
natives *zoncor*, and are well supplied with bomb
and cannon, and other pieces of artillery. On
the angles of the ramparts which command the
entrance into both harbours are two turrets,
formerly intended for the purpose of watching
the vessels which entered and left the harbour.
At present, the entrances to these are closed
with two marble slabs, one bearing an inscription to the memory of Admiral Sir A. Ball,
once governor of Malta, below which are interred his remains surrounded by an iron railing ; and the other in memory of Sir Ralph
Abercrombie, whose embalmed body is enclosed
in a barrel within the turret, just as it was
brought from Aboukir. From this circumstance,
the ramparts to the west are called after the
name of the former, *Ball's bastion*, and those to
the east, *Abercrombie's bastions*.

From the watch-tower surmounting the fort,

vessels may be seen at a great distance; the quality of the sail in sight is marked by different signals, and the points which they are coming may be known by the position in which these signs are placed, on a stand prepared for the purpose. This custom existed in the time of the Order, and is continued to the present day. Men-of-war are signified by two balls suspended on a small pole, a packet by one, and a Merchant vessel by a small square white flag.

The treble row of magazines, nineteen on each story, now forming a barrack for two regiments of the line, was erected, under the auspices of the Grandmaster Emmanuel Pinto, and intended for storehouses of ammunition for the Order, and a safe asylum for females in case of a siege. These magazines are bomb proof, and are built within the walls, under the western wing of the Fort, from a design by the Cavalier Tignè. The terrace of this building is well paved, and forms a delightful walk, enjoying an extensive view of the sea. In the square, in front of the barracks, is a fine fountain, surmounted by four large stone shells, from which the water was formerly made to spring. Over the two gates which open the descent to the square, were placed the arms of the Grandmaster Pinto, surrounded with warlike trophies and other ornaments. Those on the northwestern side have been thrown down; but those opposite, towards the town, are still to be seen; though somewhat destroyed by the hand of time.

The fort of St. Elmo is at present garrisoned by English Artillery, and a small detachment of infantry. The quarters which they occupy are healthy; those on the walls are open to the air, and those below are built with spacious corridors along the ranges of rooms. There was a small chapel in the fort, which is now used for a different purpose. The light-house which rises from one of the angles, has lately been improved by the English Government.

Since the year 1565, when St. Elmo unhappily fell into the hands of the Turks, but was afterwards retaken by the knights, the fort was seized upon by various priests and malcontents amounting to between three and four hundred persons. This event took place during the short reign of the Grandmaster Francis Ximenes de Texada; but the conspirators were soon obbliged to abandon their position. On being seized by the Bailiff de Rohan, who had the charge of the attack, some were executed, whilst others were either banished or imprisoned.

The next object of interest to which I would direct the attention of the traveller is the

GOVERNOR'S PALACE.

PALACE.

It was the original intention to erect a residence for the Grandmaster of the Order on the site now occupied by the Auberge de Castile; but P. de Monte preferred the present spot, situated on the most level part of the town, with a spacious square in the front, called Piazza San Giorgio. The ensemble of the exterior presents nothing striking, the whole forming a pile of unadorned architecture, about three hundred feet square, surrounded on every side by four of the principal streets, and almost enclosed on three with a line of open and covered balconies. It has two principal entrances on the front, each opening into an open court, and one in the centre of the three remaining sides.

The interior of the Palace was very much improved by the Grandmaster Emmanuel Pinto. It consists of a lower and upper story, each containing a range of appartments running round the building, and another transversely, which divides the space within into two almost equal divisions. The court to the left is by far the most spacious, and is surrounded by a portico formed with arches, covering a fountain opposite the entrance, surmounted with a statue of Neptune fixed in the wall behind. In the other yard, which communicates with the former, is a fountain, the Government Printing

I

Office, the Office of the Comptroller of Charitable institutions, that of Hypothecations, of the Crown Advocate, of the Chief Secretary to Government, and that of the Executive Police, the Military Secretary's Office, and the old armoury.

The upper story consists of numerous elegant apartments and spacious halls, embellished with views commemorative of the battles of the Order, executed by Matteo de Lecce. Some of the paintings are of a superior workmanship, and will well repay more than a cursory examination. Among the several masters whose genius adorns these walls are, Caravaggio, Giuseppe d' Arpino and Cavalier Favray. In the Waiting Room, at the end of the Hall, as you ascend the chief stairs, are to be seen productions of Busuttil and Caruana, two Maltese artists. Their principal pieces represent St. George and the Dragon, St. Michael, St. Peter, Mary Magdalen, and Æneas. Most of the very ancient paintings in the Palace were placed here by the Grandmaster Zondadari, and are chiefly scriptural illustrations.

During Sir Gaspard Le Marchant's administration, the corridors of this Palace were paved with marble in mosaic, and subsequently, the principal stair-case was also paved with the same costly material.

In the corridor leading to the armoury is the entrance to a room hung with tapestry of very superior workmanship. The drawings on these hangings represent scenes in India and Africa, and a great collection of natural history. The article was brought from France about 150 years since, yet the colours still look fresh and new. This elegant room is now exclusively devoted for the sittings of the Government Council.

The most interesting sight in this building, and one well worthy the attention of the stranger is the Armoury. This occupies a large saloon, extending the whole length of the building, containing the armour, and a great many warlike weapons belonging to the Knights of Malta, with numerous trophies of their splendid victories. The principal musketry was manufactured at the Tower of London, and placed here by the English Government, when that of the Order was removed. The number of regular arms, which up to two years were shewn in this place were as follows :

19,555 Muskets and bayonets.

 1,000 Pistols.

30,000 Boarding pikes.

    90 Complete coats of armour for mounted knights.

   450 Cuirasses, casques, and gauntlets for infantry.

The last mentioned armour is arranged along the upper part of the room in regular order, with their respective shields, on which is portrayed the white cross of the Order on a red field. The armour for the mounted cavaliers and men-at-arms is of different kinds, some banished, and others painted black and varnished. The complete suits are placed upright on stands, and posted up along the rows of muskets, at certain distance from each other, looking like so many sentinels, and giving a sombre appearance to the whole room. A trial was once made of the force of resistance of one of these suits, and several musket-balls were discharged against it at sixty yards distance, which only produced a very shallow concavity. This piece of armour is still preserved with the rest. The muskets and bayonets however have been lately removed.

At one end of the room is a complete coat of black armour standing about seven feet high, and three and a half wide. It is not very probable that this has been often used; the helmet alone weighs thirty seven pounds.

Close by the above is an open case, in which may be seen many curious specimens of musketry, pistols, swords daggers, &c. chiefly trophies taken by the knights in their engagement with the Turks. The sword of the famous Algerine general Dragut is preserved among these spoils.

Before this case is a cannon made of tarred rope, bound round a thin lining of copper, and covered on the outside with a coat of plaster painted black. This is a curious specimen of ancient warfare, and was taken from the Turks during one of their attacks upon the city of Rhodes. It is about five feet long, and three inches in the calibre.

At the other extremity of the room is the complete armour of the Grandmaster Alofio Wignacourt, beautifully enchased with gold; above which is a drawing of the same, armed cap-a-pie, a copy from a masterpiece of the famous Caravaggio which is in the Dining-room.

Several parts of the walls are covered with many curious specimens of ancient warlike implements. Here one may see cross bows, maces, coats of mail, javelins, battle-axes, and various other instruments of bloodshed and death, which were wielded in days of yore by those who long since have finished their warfare, and now sleep silently in the grave.

A man of reflection cannot fail to be affected with the vanity of ambition, as he examines these relics of the prowess of bygone years. Is this all that remains of so much anxiety and love of power? " How mean are these ostentatious methods of bribing the vote of fame, and purchasing a little posthumous renown!" " How are the mighty fallen, and the weapons of war perished! " Of the one it may be said :

"A heap of dust alone remains of thee,
'Tis all thou art, and all the pride shall be."

while the other serves for the decoration of a palace, and the momentary entertainment of a passing stranger.

On the most elevated part of the Palace is the Torretta; a small quadrangular tower, from whence vessels of war are signalized. In the lower part of this building were formerly preserved the treasures of the Order; among which was the sword, shield, and golden belt of Philip II. King of Spain, sent by him as a present to the Grandmaster La Valette. These articles, carried away by the French, during their occupation in 1798-1800, are now at the National Museum in Paris.

I must not take leave of the Palace without leading the stranger to the Government chapel; but in order to this, he must follow me from the highest to the lowest part of the building, in a secluded spot, to the left of the chief entrance. It is a long room capable of accomodating about three hundred persons and fitted up with pews, the greater part of which belong to persons employed by the Government, and the remainder let out to hire. The only part of the chapel where a stranger may find a sitting, without intruding upon the premises of another, is the end of the room, where hearing is almost impossible. Here is now the office of the Land Revenue.

After having examined all that is interesting in the Governor's Palace, we shall next notice the

AUBERGES OF THE KNIGHTS OF MALTA.

There was a palace or inn for each language of the Order where all the members, whether knights, serving brothers, professed or novices, equally eat. The Commanders seldom went thither; indeed those who were possessed of a commandery worth two thousand Maltese dollars could not be admitted; neither could the servants-at-arms, if they had a commandery worth one thousand crowns. The chief of each inn was called the *Pilier*, and he received either a sum of money, or the equivalent in grain from the public treasury, for the provision of the members of his inn. The rest of the expenses were paid by himself, for which he was indemnified by the first vacant dignity in his language.

In these edifices the knights of each nation not only eat, but assembled together for the pnrposes of consultation, and the transaction of business. Such as preferred residing in their respective inns to having private houses of their own were permitted to do so; the same privilege was enjoyed by the brother chaplains, and the brother pages, in tho service of the Order.

The superior of every language was dignified with a distinctive title, to which were annexed certain functions, which we shall notice in our description of each inn.

Auberge de Provence.

The superior of this auberge was denominated the Grand Commander; who, by virtue of his office was perpetual president of the common treasury, comptroller of the accounts, superintendent of shores, governor of the arsenal, and master of the ordinance. He had the nomination (subject to the approbation of the Grandmaster and council) of all officers from the different languages; and to this he added the power of appointing persons to the various places of trust in the church of St. John, and in the Infirmary.

The Auberge de Provence is situated in Strada Reale; it is a fine building, with a plain but imposing facade. The lower apartments are at present appropriated for the sale of goods by auction, the office of one of the public auctioneers, &c.; the upper rooms are let to the Malta Union Club.

Besides the chapel which this language owned in the church of St. John, it possessed another separate church, as did also several of the other languages. That of Santa Barbara belonged to the Knights of Provence; it is situated a little higher up than the auberge, in the same street, on the opposite side. This chapel is at present made use of by the inhabitants.

The next in order is the

Auberge d' Auvergne.

The head of this inn was called the Grand Marshal; he had the military command over all the Order, excepting the grand crosses or their lieutenants, the chaplains, and other persons of the Grandmaster's household. He entrusted the standard of the Order to that knight whom he judged most worthy of such distinction. He had the right of appointing the principal equery; and when at sea, not only commanded the general of the gallies, but the grand admiral himself.

This auberge is even more simple in its structure than the former; and occupies a site opposite the side square of St. John's church, in Strada Reale. It is at present appropriated in its upper floor for the civil courts; the tribunals of appeal and commerce, as also for the criminal court, and in the ground floor for the courts of magistrates of judicial police.

Auberge d' Italie.

The superior of this language was styled the Admiral. In the Grand Marshal's absence, he had the command of the soldiery equally with the seamen; he also appointed the comptroller and secretary of the arsenal, and when he demanded to be named to the generalship of the gallies, the Grandmaster was obliged to propose him to the council, which was at liberty to appoint or to reject him at pleasure.

This auberge is situated in Strada Mercanti, opposite to the Auberge de Castile. Over the entrance is a bronze bust of the Grandmaster Carafa, with his coat of arms and many trophies and ornaments of white marble, said to have been cut from a large pillar which once stood in the temple of Proserpine in the Città Notabile. Below the bust is the following inscription:

Gregorio Carafae Principi Optimo
belli pacisque artibus maximo
post Ottomanicam classem ductu suo
bis ad Hellespontum profligatam
relatasque XI quinqueremium manubi as
ad summum Hierosolymitani Ordinis
regimen evecto
Itala equestris natio
Magistrali munere saeculo
amplius viduata
augustam hanc effigiem
reparatae majestatis indicem D. D.
A. D. MDCLXXXIII.

To this language belonged the small church of Santa Catarina which adjoins it, having a small platform in front, enclosed with an iron railing. The principal painting in this church is that representing Sta. Catarina's martyrdom; a good original by the Cav. Calabrese.

The Auberge d' Italie is at present occupied by the Royal Engineers' Arsenal, and the archives where the acts and records of deceased notaries are kept. Opposite to this building is the

Auberge de Castile.

The chief of this inn was dignified with the title of the Grand Chancellor. It belonged to his office always to present the Vicechancellor to the council; and his presence was likewise necessary whenever any *bulls* were stamped with the great seal.

This is the largest auberge in the city, and occupies a very delightful situation close under the walls of the ditch, commanding an extensive view of the country beyond. It has three entrances; that to the front is ascended by a grand semicircular pyramidal staircase, and is surmounted with a great display of ornamental sculpture consisting chiefly of warlike trophies, arms, musical instruments, &c. In the centre is a marble bust of the Grandmaster Pinto, with the following inscription carved on the base:

Em. ac Seren. Princ.
F. D. Emmanuel Pinto
De Fonseca,
Magisteri sui
Anno IV.

To the knights of this language appartained the church of St. James in Strada Mercanti; a very neat specimen of architecture, ornamented in a very chaste and simple style. This church, though but seldom used by them, is also in the hands of the Maltese.

The Auberge de Castile is at present occupied by officers of the English Garrison.

Auberge de France.

The superior of this inn, during the existance of the Order, was called the Grand Hospitalier. He had the direction of the hospital, and appointed the Overseer and Prior to the infirmary, and also ten writers to the council. The officers who filled these employments were changed every two years.

The Auberge de France is situated in Strada Mezzodì, and is a plain, but commodious building. It is at present the residence of the Commissary General.

Auberge d' Aragona.

The title of the superior of this inn was the Draper, or the Grand Conservator. He was charged with every thing relative to the Con-

servatory, to the clothing, and to the purchase
of all necessary articles, not only for the troops,
but also for the hospitals.

This building occupies a small square, with
the front opening into Strada Vescovo; and
is now the residence of the Bishop of Gibraltar.

Auberge of England,
and
Anglo-Bavarian.

The head of this establishment was dignified
with the title of the Turcopolier; he had the
command over the cavalry, and the guards stationed on the coast.

While the Language of England existed
their inn was the building which fronts the
square before the small church of *Sta. Catarina
of the Italians* on the one side, and Strada Reale on the other.

The new Theatre was lately constructed
on the site formerly occupied by this Auberge.

After the Reformation, when all the English
commanderies were confiscated by order of
Henry VIII. this language ceded up its rights,
and was succeeded by the Anglo-Bavarian,
whose inn stands on the platform of St. Lazarus,
facing the entrance to the Quarantine harbour.
This building is very plain in its structure;
and is at present occupied by the officers of the
B.i.ish garrison.

Auberge of Germany.

The Grand Bailiff of the Order was the title given to the superior of this inn. His jurisdiction comprised all the fortifications of the Castle of Gozo.

This auberge was pulled down in the year 1839 and on its place is built the Protestant Collegiate Church of St. Paul. The first stone of this temple was laid by H. late M. Queen Dowager Adelaide on the 20th of March of that year, in which she sojourned in the Island.

Having noticed all the Inns of the Order we shall next direct the attention of the stranger to

ST. JOHN'S CHURCH.

This edifice holds the first rank among the numerous churches and convents of Malta. It was built during the reign of the Grandmaster La Cassiere, about the year 1576, and was subsequently enriched by the donations of the Grandmasters who succeeded him; especially by Nicholas Cotoner and Emmanuel Pinto, and likewise by several of the sovereigns of Europe. The church was consecrated by D. Ludovico Torres, Archibishop of Monreal; and at the first general chapter held at Malta a separate chapel was assigned to the knights of each language. The facade seems very clumsy, and the ensemble quite monotonous. The building which adjoins the church on the right was formerly the residence of the Prior of the Order, that to the left was tenanted by others of the clergy belonging to the establishment, and includes several apartments, in which were preserved the treasures of the church. These were mostly all seized by the French during their short occupation of the island.

The interior is of an oblong form ; the uppermost part, which forms the choir, is ornamented with an admirable piece of sculpture in white marble, on a raised base, representing the baptism of Christ by St. John, in two large figures. The above was from a design by the famous Maltese artist Melchior Gafà, and completed after his death by Bernini. The semicircular roof which covers the nave is adorned with paintings illustrative of the life of the above mentioned saint, by the Cavalier Mathias Preti, surnamed the Calabrese, by whom most of the paintings of the church were executed. This distinguished artist is buried before the entrance into the vestry. He died in January 1739.

These paintings, of admirable excellence, representing the life of the Precursor, were greatly damaged, and in many parts they are almost entirely destroyed. The Government lately resolved on restoring them, and entrusted the difficult work to Sig. J. C. Cortis, Maltese, a distinguished pupil of the Roman school. The work is now in course of execution. A sum of about £ 3000 will be expended by the Government for the restoration, not including the gilding of the vault, which work is to be carried out by another Maltese, Signor Antonio Gauci.

The pavement is composed of sepulchral slabs worked in mosaic with various coloured marble; many of them contain jasper, agate, and other precious stones, the cost of which must have been very great. Some of these cover the graves of the knights, and other servants of the Order, and bear each an appropriate epitaph, or rather a panegyric on the virtues of the deceased.

The grand altar which stands at the uppermost part of the nave is very sumptuous and deserves notice on account of the various coloured marble, and other valuable stones of which it is constructed. Before it, on either side, on a raised pavement, stands a chair covered with a rich canopy of crimson velvet: that to the left is occupied by the bishop, and the one on the right is destined for the sovereign of the island, over which is placed the escutcheon of Great Britain.

The chapels of the different languages of the Order, which run parallel with the nave form the two aisles, and are very splendidly decorated. The roofs are constructed in the shape of a dome in the interior, and very profusely carved with different ornaments in alto-rilievo as also are the walls. The whole was gilded during the reigns of Raphael and Nicholas Cotoner, as appears from an inscription over the entrance on the west side of the building. The arches of these chapels correspond on both sides, and leave their interior quite exposed to view as you pass down the nave.

The first arch, on the right hand as you enter the church forms a passage into the Oratory or Chapel of the Crucifixion. This was sent apart for the worship of the clergy during the existence of the Order. There are several fine paintings in this chapel, especially one behind the altar of the Beheading of St. John, the work, of Michael-Angelo Caravaggio. The roof is remarkable chaste, and is not so profuse in gilded ornaments as many other parts of the building. From this chapel a flight of stairs leads down to a subterraneous appartment, where there is a room in which stands a rustic altar. The floor coveres several vaults, which were destined for the interment of Commanders of the Order.

The second arch covers the chapel of the Portuguese Knights. Over the altar is a drawing of St. James; and on the side walls are two other paintings representing some traditionary scenes in the life of the apostle. In this chapel are two mausoleums: one of Emmanuel Pinto, surmounted with his portrait in mosaic, and a large marble representation of Fame; the other, of Manoel de Vilhena, is by far the most costly. The whole of the latter is bronze sustained by two lions of the same material. On a table beneath his bust is an alto-rilievo group, representing the Grandmaster giving directions concerning the construction of Fort Manoel, the plan of which is spread out beforehim by one of the knights. The accompanying sketches will give some idea of these monuments.

The third arch forms the entrance into the church from the eastern side, and contains no altar. The roof and walls, however, are carved and gilded in the same manner with the rest.

The fourth arch leads into the chapel of the Spanish Knights. Over the altar is a painting of St. George; those of the side walls represent the trial and martyrdom of St. Lawrence. In this chapel are the mausoleums of four Grandmasters; Martin de Redin, Raphael Cotoner, Perellos y-Roccafoull, and Nicholas Cotoner. the two last mentioned are very grand. That of Roccafoull is surmounted by a fine copper bust, with a figure on each side as large as life, one representing Justice, and the other Charity. The whole is adorned with warlike weapons and armour cut in white marble, and exhibiting a very imposing appearance. That of Nicholas Cotoner is equally grand; the monument is sustained by two slaves in a bending posture, one representing a Turk and the other an African; a very graphic delineation of the false

EMMANUEL DE VILHENA.
Grand Master.

RAYMONDO DE PERELLOS ET ROCCAFUL M.M.
Grand Master.

views of Gospel liberty which formed the basis of all the crusades.

This monument of great beauty and of most finished execution in the sculpture of marble with which it is profusely decorated, was also the work of the celebrated Maltese Artist, Melchiorre Gafà.

The fifth arch leads into the chapel of the Language of Provence. The paintings over the altar represent the torture of St. Sebastian; and the side drawings are also illustrations of some parts of the same history. The mausoleum of the Grandmaster Gessan is very simple, consisting of a black marble inscription surmounted with a marble bust.

The sixth and uppermost arch leads into the small chapel of the Virgin. This, however, is not open to the nave, being covered with the benches which form the choir. The altar in this chapel is surrounded with a balaustrade of massy silver posts, placed along a row of low marble pillars which extend the whole breadth of the room. A famous painting, representing the "Lady of Philermos," and placed over the Island, was taken away by the last Grandmaster F. Hompesch, during the French invasion, and presented by him to the Emperor of Russia.—Another picture of little value was temporarily hang up instead of the other painting, but was lately replaced by another one, the work of Cav. Gagliardi of Rome. Enclosed

within this, on the side walls, are three silver
plates containing the three following inscriptions
with a bundle af keys suspended to each. These
as may be seen from the writing, were taken as
trophies.

1.

Deiparae Virgini ac Divo
Baptistae tutelari
Castri Parsava in Pelo-
poneso a militibus Hierosonis, vi-
capto sub F. Ia. Dublot viverio
triremium praefecto anno
salu. humae. MDCI. die XVIII. Aug. mensis
F. Alofius Vignacurtius M.
Magister tunc primum sui
regiminis annum agens has oppidi
claves ac signa Turcica memoriae
ac pietatis ergo consecravit.

2.

Anno post captum Passava
ejusdem viverii ejusdemq'.
mensis Aug. felicitate ibid'.
orto jam sole excisis portis ac
Magno militum impetu muris per
scalas superatis capto etiam
Hadrymeto urbes in Africa vulgo
Hamametu idem Mag. Alofius eid.
Em. Virgini Matri uc D. Baptistae
quorum auspiciis haec gesta
sunt pro gratiarum actione
hoc monumentum posuit.

MARC ANTONIO ZONDADARIO.

Grand Master.

NICOLA COTONER.

Grand Master.

3.

Duo Castra ad custodiam
Corinthiaci sinus in ejus
facib'. a barbaris ultimo
constructa idem Alofius
quo matris tractu sociali bello ad-
versus Selimum Milesolim pugnave-
rat, nunc M. Mag. an. sui principat.' III.
et Fascanio Cambriano classis prefec-
to a suis capta diripuit. Ingentib'. ad
LLX tormentis inter alia huc inde ad-
vectis tantae igitur victoriae monumen-
ta S. Victori cui auspiciis die illi sacro eam
acceptam referat ac Deiparae dedicavit.

To the left hand, on entering the church, is a splendid copper mausoleum of the Grandmaster Zondadari. The whole is supported by a marble base, and flanked with two fine pillars of the same material. The metal statue of the knight, as large as life in a reclining posture, and the various ornaments which surround it are very grand and may be regarded as a first rate production of art.

Walking down the left aisle, the first arch leads into the vestry, in which are several paintings; among them are full length portraits of the Grandmaster Pinto, La Cassiere, Perellos, and Nicolas Cotoner.

The second chapel is that of the Knights of Austria. The alter piece represents the Adoration of the Wise Men; the pieces on the side walls illustrate the Murder of the Innocents, and the birth of our Saviour.

These fine paintings are the works of the celebrated Maltese Artist, G. Erardi.

The third arch form the western entry into the church. The walls of this recess are covered with small and neat sculpture.

The fourth chapel is that of the Italian Knights; the walls are ornamented much in the same manner as the former. There are in this chapel two fine drawings of St. Jerome and Mary Magdalen, said to be the work of the famous Caravaggio. The painting over the altar represent St. Catherine. One of the finest and most valued works of Matthias Preti. The only mausoleum here is that of the Grandmaster Carafa, which is partly of marble and partly of copper. On the wall behind the bust is a prospective view in alto-rilievo of the entry of several gallies into the harbour of Malta.

The next chapel is that of the language of the Knights of France. The conversion of St. Paul over the altar, is a fine piece. The drawings on the side walls represent the holy family and St. John in the desert. In this chapel are the monuments of two Grandmasters, and one of the Prince Ludovico Philip d'Orleans, who was interred here in the year 1808.

The sixth and last chapel is that of the Knights of Bavaria. Over the altar is a drawing of St. Michael and the Dragon, and on one side of the wall another of his miraculous appearance. The other side forms a small chapel in a recess, enclosed with a brass balustrade, dedicated to St. Carlo Boromeo. This was used by the English Knights of the Order.

In this chapel, an old statue in wood representing St. John, is remarkable. It belonged to the famous *Caracca* or Galley of the Order; it was the custom of the Knights to assemble before the statue in order to implore victory, before their national engagements.

From this chapel a staircase leads down to an underground apartment, in which are the tombs of several Grandmasters. Here is interred L' Isle Adam, the first commander of the Order in Malta. The remainder are those of La Valette, Wignacourt, La Cassiere, Cardinal Verdala, Ludovico Mendes de Vasconcellos, Pietro de Monte, and Martin de Garzes. The remains of these are chiefly deposited in sarcophagi of Malta stone, with marble or bronze covers, on some of which are carved full-length images of the deceased. On the pavement are three marble slabs with inscriptions to the memory of Claudius de la Sengle, Petrino de Ponte, and Ioan de Omedes; who, together with several of the above mentioned, were removed to this cemetery after the building of the church.

On particular days the interior of the building is covered with a rich tapestry,which gives it a very splendid appearance. This article was presented as a gift to the church by the Grandmaster Perellos.

St. John's Church is one of the most conspicuous monuments of Christianity. Its pavement is of the highest historical importance, containing the history of three centures of glory and greatness. Under the Order the temple was richly decorated with silver ornaments, which were carried off by the French together with those of the Cathedral Church of the magnificent silver service of the renowned Hospital of Malta. On the overthrow of the Order, Napoleon made over this Church to Mons. Labini, the then Bishop of this Island. Since that time the chapter of this diocese officiate in the Conventual Church of the Knights of St. John, which is now administered by the Government, and bears the title of Co-Cathedral.

An old Cemetery will be observed by the visitor on the right side of this Temple. A pyramid is erected over the tombs, recording the glorious deeds of many heroes who were killed in battle. Under the slabs are deposited the remains of the Knights who fell during the memorable siege of Malta in the year 1565.

Besides the church already mentioned, there are three others in the city which belong to the Government; viz. the Church of the Jesuits in

Strada Mercanti, Di Liesse on the Marina, and St. Rocco in Strada St. Ursola. The former of these we may have occasion to mention in our remarks on the Jesuit's college now the Government University. The church of the Liesse belonged to the Knights of France. The walls of this building are adorned with gifts devoted to the Virgin, the fulfillment of vows made in time of affliction, in order to obtain her commiseration. The boatmen hold this church in peculiar veneration.

The two parish churches of the city are those of St. Domenico and St. Paolo; the former is connected with a monastery of Dominician friars; the latter is a collegiate church situated in the street of the same name. The other monkish orders are those of the Augustinians, Carmelites, Franciscans, and the *Minori Osservanti* or Reformed Franciscans; all of which have churches connected with their respective convents. Besides these, there are two large nunneries, one of Ursuline and the other of Sta. Catarina nuns. Two other churches in the city, one dedicated to Sta. Lucia, and the other called delle Anime (of the Souls in Purgatory) belong to the public. The Greek Catholics have also a parish church, dedicated to St. Maria, in Strada Vescovo. Several of these churches are ornamented with fine paintings.

It is calculated that the number of ordained priests and friars in the islands of Malta and

K

Gozo exceeds one thousand; these are supported from the revenues of their respective
churches and convents, the contributions of
the people, and the money paid in masses for
the living and the dead. Beside the above there
are many *Abbati* preparing for ordination who
are considered a part of the ecclesiastical establishment of the island.

In the month of February, in the year 1823,
a very mournful event took place in one of the
convents of Malta, no less dreadful in its effects
than that of the Black hole of Calcutta. The
circumstance was as follows :

It was usual in this island, on the last days
of the Carnival, to collect together, from Valletta and from the three cities on the other
side of the harbour, as many boys of the lower
classes, of from 8 to 15 years of age, as chose
to attend,—to form them into a procession,
and to take them out to Floriana or elsewhere,
where, after attending service in the church a
collation of bread and fruit (provided from funds
partly given by Government and partly by bene-
ficient individuals) was distributed to them,—and
this with the view of keeping them out of the
riot and confusion of the Carnival in the streets
of the cities. The arrangement of this procession was under the control of the Ecclesiastical
Directors of the Institution for teaching the
Catechism. It appears that this procession had
taken place on the 10th Feb. that the children

went to Floriana, and from thence returned to the church of the *Minori Osservanti* in Valletta, and that the bread was on that day distributed in the Convent of that Order without any accident or confusion.

On the 11th the procession was formed as usual, proceeded to Floriana, and returned to the church of the *Minori Osservanti*, and the bread was to be distributed, as on the preceding day, in the same convent. Unfortunately however, the ceremony had been protracted to a later hour than usual, and it appears (the Carnival being over,) that a multitude of boys and full grown people, passing by the church and knowing that bread was to be distributed, mixed with the children in the church with the view of sharing it with them.

The boys were to enter the corridor of the convent from the door of the vestry of the church, and were to be let out through the opposite door of the convent in Strada St. Ursola, where the bread was to be distributed; and it had been customary, when they were collected in the corridor, to lock the door of the vestry, for the purpose of preventing those boys who had received the share of the bread from entering the second time into the corridor.

On the door of the vestry, however, being thrown open on the present occasion, which took place about sun-set, after the entrance of the boys, who originally attended the proces-

sion, and who could not have exceeded one
hundred, a whole multitude of men and boys,
who had subsequently entered the church, forced themselves into the corridor to an unknown
extent, and pressed upon the foremost, pushing
them gradually to the other end of the corridor
where the door was only half open, with the
view of letting out one at a time.

As soon as the people had all entered the
corridor, the vestry door was as usual locked,
and, though there was one lamp lighted in the
corridor, it appears, by some accident, to have
been put out—thus leaving this immense crowd
entirely in the dark; and there being unfortunately a flight of eight steps within the half
closed door, at the opposite end of the corridor
the crowd behind, who pressed upon the foremost, forced the boys down the steps, who fell
one upon the other, thus unfortunately shoaking
up the half-shut door at the bottom (which
opened inwards,) and adding to the distress.

The shrieks of the children were soon heard
by the persons employed in the distribution of
the bread which they had commenced issuing,
and by the inhabitants of the neighbourhood,—
and it appears that every aid was immediately
given. Some persons, after endeavouring in
vain to get the boys out of the half closed door,
rushed into the church and got the keys of the
vestry door, which was then opened ; — while
others entered the corridor from the vestry

passed through the crowd to the other end, and broke down the door at the bottom of the steps; —but unfortunately their exertions where not in time to save the unhappy sufferers.

Many, however, were taken out fainting and soon recovered; others apparently lifeless were afterwards brought to their senses; but, sad to relate, one hundred and ten boys of from 8 to 15 years of age perished on this occasion from suffocation, by being pressed together in so small a space, or trampled upon.

HOSPITALS.

The present Military Hospital, situated at the lower extremity of Strada Mercanti, was formerly the public building used for the reception of the sick by the Knights of Malta. It is a very commodious edifice, containing many ranges of rooms, disposed in excellent order for the free circulation of air, with a spacious court, in the centre of which is a good fountain. During the existence of the Order, this establishment was open to strangers as well as to the citizens, for whom suitable accomodations were provided. The sick were regularly attended by the knights in person, provided with medicines and medical assistance free of expense, and their food served up to them in vessels of silver. Here also was a provision made for foundings.

The direction of this institution, after the Grandmaster, was committed to the chief Hospitalier, which dignity appartained to the French knights. To him belonged the election of the Overseer of the Infirmary, the Prior, and other ministers. The Overseer generally resided in the Hospital; to the Prior, was committed the charge of the spiritual concerns of the patients, and the other ecclesiastical servants helped in assisting the sick, and in celebrating the sacrament in different wards. To the right hand, on entering the chief gate of the Hospital, was the Pharmacy of the establishment, well supplied with all kinds of drugs and medicines. This is used for the same purpose at the present day.

On the arrival of the French, they seized upon all the plate which was to be found in the establishment, and converted the building into a Military Hospital. The inhabitants being obliged to demand another, the Nunnery of Sta. Maddalena was given them, the nuns promptly yielding up their residence for the purpose, some of whom retired into the monastery of Sta. Catarina, and others went to their homes.

Close by, was the cemetry for all persons who died in the Hospital, which adjoins a small church called the *Church of the Cemetery*, founded by the Commendatore Fra Giorgio Nibbia, who is himself buried there. Upon a part of the locality which formed the burial-ground is now built a semicircular building, set apart for disection, and practical lessons in anatomy, to the students who attend the government University. By the side of this is a very extensive charnel-house, containing many thousand sculls and human bones, which have been dug up from time to time out of the cemetery.

Close to the above was the public Female Hospital, founded in the year 1646 by the Lady Catarina Scoppi Senese, who bequeathed the building to the public, and endowed it with all her wealth. This institution which existed till the year 1850 was likewise under the direction of two knights of the Order, who were called Commissioners.

Opposite this building was the public Male Hospital, which in the time of the Order, as I have mentioned above, was a Nunnery of *The Penitents*, dedicated to Sta. Maria Maddalena. Whilst this establishment existed, by order of the Pope, it was partly supported by the fifth portion of the inheritance of prostitutes. The church which adjoined it was made use of as a ward for the wounded, and such as have broken limbs. This building was lately converted into an orphan asylum, and annexed to which are the Industrial and Normal Primary Schools of Valletta. Both Hospitals had not all the accomodations, they were therefore lately removed to a more spacious building at Floriana, of which we shall speak hereafter.

Opposite the Military Hospital is another large building, which is at present occupied by

private families. The part to the right was formerly called *La Camerata,* where a number of
the more pious knights were accustomed to
reside, and where they assembled together at
stated hours for devotion. The left division
called *la Lingerie,* was set apart as a magazine
for the linen and other articles required for the
service of the Hospital. Here also the bedding
and clothing of the patients were washed. This
building was erected in the year 1593 under the
Grandmaster Cardinal Verdala, and subsequently repaired during the reign of the Grandmaster
Lascaris. In the *Camerata* was after established
the College of St. Paul directed by the Jesuits
which was transferred from Città Vecchia in the
year 1852.

That old edifice having been demolished, a
vast building was constructed by the late Bishop Casolani for the accomodation of the lower
clases of the people.

MONTE DI PIETA'
or
PUBLIC PAWN BROKERY.

This institution occupies a large building in
Strada Mercanti, opposite the house called *Il
Banco dei Giurati.* It was originally established in the year 1507, and like all institutions
of the sort in other parts of Europe, particularly at Rome, with the object of affording pe-

cuniary relief to the distressed at reasonable
interest, thereby preventing them from having
recourse to usurious contracts. Any sum of
money, however small, is advanced to appli-
cants on the security of property given in
pawn, such as gold, silver, and other precious
articles, or wearing apparel, whether worn or
new. The period of the loan is for three years
on pawns of the first description, and never
more than two on those of the latter, renewa-
ble at the option of the parties, who are also at
liberty to redeem their pawns at any time within the period on payment of interest in proportion. The rate of interest now charged is 5 per
cent. per annum. The unclaimed pawns at the
expiration of the period, are sold by public
auction, and the residue of the proceeds, after
deducting the sum due to the institution, is
payable to the person producing the respective
tickets. Of the accomodations thus afforded
by the Monte not unfrequently persons in better circumstances have availed for any momentary exigency, and in this way considerable
sums have been advanced. Till the year 1787
the operations of this institution were conducted by means of money borrowed at a moderate
interest, and by funds acquired by donations,
&c. But the Grandmaster Rohan authorized
the consolidation of the funds of the Monte di
Pietà with those of the Monte di Redenzione,
another institution, equally national founded in

the year 1607 by private donations and bequests
for the philantrophic object of rescuing from
slavery any of the natives who might fall
into the hands of the Mohammedans not having
means of ransom. As this institution had larger
funds (mostly in landed property) than it actually required to meet all demands, the act of
consolidation proved of the greatest advantage
to the Monte di Pietà. Thus united the two
institutions, with the new title of Monte di
Pietà e Redenzione, conducted their separate
duties under the superintendence of a board
consisting of a President and eight Commissaries, till the expulsion of the Order of St. John
from Malta, which happened in the year 1798.
The French Republicans by whom the island
was then occupied stripped the Monte of every
article whether in money or pawns, and the loss
sustained by the institution on that unfortunate
occasion amounted nearly to £ 35,000 sterling,
including the share of the proprietors of pawns
in as much as the advance they received on
that security never exceeded one half or two-
thirds of the value of the articles pawned. It
is needless to state that not a shilling of this
sum was repaid by the French Government
after the occupation of the island by the English.

When the British forces took possession of
Valletta in September 1800, it was one of
the first cares of the head of the Government

to see this useful institution resume its operations; accordingly a new board was elected,
and about four thousands pounds advanced to
them (without interest) from the local treasury.
A loan was opened to which individuals did not
hesitate to contribute when they were assured
that the institution considered itself bound to
pay the loan though forming part of the amount
carried away by the French, and that in the
mean time interest would be paid on it. The
Monte possessing landed property to a much
greater amount could never refuse such an act
of justice. Happily the cessation of slavery
having put an end to the old charge for ran-
some, enabled the institution to devote its revenues to the payment of interest on the old loan
to the extinction of part of the capital, to the
improvement of its property, and for the last
fourteen years, to assign a subsidy in aid of
the expense of the House of Industry.

The Administration of the Monte di Pietà e
Redenzione was by a Minute of the Governor
dated the 27th December 1837, vested from
the 1st January 1838, in the Commitee of the
Government Charitable Institutions; instead of
the former board consisting of a President and
six Commissaries. A Saving Bank was annexed to the Monte di Pietà, in 1833, which
istitution has produced a very effect in an eco-
nomical point of view.

GOVERNMENT UNIVERSITY.

Formerly the Jesuits' College.

It was during a very tumultuous and seditious time in the era of the Knights of Malta that the Jesuits were called in by Bishop Gargallo to support him against the power of the Order. This learned body of men soon gained the same ascendancy in Malta as in every other place where they have ever been established. In order to provide them with a permanent settlement in the island, the above prelate erected for them the present church and college, the foundation of which was laid on the 12th of November 1593, during the reign of the Grandmaster Verdala.

The Jesuits, however, did not long enjoy their power in Malta. Forty-seven years after their introduction, an affair took place which terminated in their expulsion. Some young knights, who had just ceased acting as pages, disguised themselves as Jesuits during the Carnival. This so offended the holy fathers, that they made their complaints to Lascaris and the Grandmaster immediately gave orders that some of the youths should be apprehended. This act enraged their companions, who proceeded first to the prison, the gates of which they forced, and after liberating their companions from their confinement, proceeded in a body to the college, threw the furniture out of the windows, aud compelled the Grandmaster to send the Jesuits out of the island. Eleven of them were accordingly embarked; but four contrived to secrete themselves in the city where they remained. This event occurred in the year 1639 their total expulsion did not take place until the year 1769, after which the institution became subject to the Order, and from them was transferred over to the direction of the British Government.

The university and church occupy an extensive site surrounded by four principal streets. The latter is a very regular and neatly ornamented building, containing several paintings by the Cavalier Calabrese. To the left of the southern entrance, over which is the inscription *in nomine Jesu omne genu flectatur* are two oratories. In 1803, the Governor Sir A. Ball instituted the Merchants' Bank in one angle of this edifice, which was considered as a great piece of injustice by the Maltese, who perhaps did not esteem the proceeding so much a desecration of the locality, as to delude themselves that it was an infringement on their rights. The decision of the existing government carried through the design.

The two Banks and the Exchange, together with the two other Commercial Establishments were lately united and centred in a new and elegant edifice, expressly constructed for the purpose, in Strada Reale on the plan of the

L

Maltese Architect Mr. Giuseppe Bonavia, and by contributions of the Commercial Body. The inauguration of this establishment took place on the 11th April 1857. The first floor of this building has been destined for a *Casino* (club) accessible to all persons of a respectable class. The submarine telegraph office was first established in a part of the Old Exchange but it has since been removed to a house on the Marsamuscetto bastion, and the whole building is now appropriated for the University.

The University was at different periods, subject to various changes, and the last reform which took place, and came into operation on the 1st of January 1839, was that suggested through the representations of the Commissioners sent out to examine into this institution, as well as into other grievances of the people. This change is still in full force, though it was afterwards modified in some particular circumstances.

A statute was then published with the approbation of Government, and it maintained the division of the University from the Lyceum.

The University consists now of four faculties; viz: of Philosophy and Arts, of Theology, of Law and of Medicine, and the number of professors is reduced to the following:—

Faculty af Philosophy and Arts.

1. Professor of Mathematics;
2. ———— of Logic;
3. ———— of Latin literature;
4. ———— of Italian literature;
5. ———— of English literature.

Faculty of Medicine.

1. Professor of Medicine;
2. ———— of Anatomy and Surgery;
3. ———— of Midwifery;
4. ———— of Chemistry;
5. ———— of Botany.

Faculty of Law.

1. Professor of Civil Institutes, and of the Institutes of the Law of Malta;

2. Professor of Canon Law, of the Law of Nations and of Public Law, and of Criminal Law, as regards raits penal pt. { with the application to the Island of Malta and its dependencies.

————and of Maltese Criminal Procedure and the Maltese Civil Procedure.

Faculty of Theology.

1. Professor of Dogmatical Theology;
2. ———— of Moral do.

The Lyceum is considered as a preparatory school to the University, and it consists of thirteen masterships, viz:

1. Master of Latin,

2. Master of Italian,
3. ———— of English,
4. ———— of French,
5. ———— of Hebrew,
6. ———— of ancient and modern Greek,
7. ———— of Arabic,
8. ———— of Arithmetic,
9. ———— of Geometry,
10. ———— of Navigation,
11. ———— of Caligraphy,
12. ———— of Drawing,
13. ———— of general History and Geography.

Another Lyceum was established by Sir Henry Storks in 1866 for the convenience of the inhabitants of the towns on the other side of the Grand Harbour; the extent of the instruction therein imported is more limited than in that of Valletta. There is another Lyceum in the Island of Gozo.

At the head of the whole institution there is a Rector, who has the superintendence of the University and Lyceum.

With reference to the government of the University and Lyceum, it was to be assisted by four special councils as well as by a general one.

The four special Councils were composed of every professor of the respective faculty, two non-professional members, and the Rector.

Every particular council, was to interfere directly in matters with connection with its faculty, and that of Philosophy and Arts with those concerning the Lyceum.

The general Council was composed of a professor and two non-professional members of every faculty over which presided also the Rector, but after some years the special council met only to examine the candidates for academical degrees; and in these last years the general Council very seldom was mentioned.

The government Library is separated again from the University, and is under the control of a Committee of which the Librarian serves as a secretary. The Primary Schools have been placed also under a special Director, with the title of Director and Professor of primary education, who was charged to introduce in this institution a more recent plan of early education as carried on in the schools of the United Kingdom of Great Britain.

PUBLIC LIBRARY.

The building which encloses the Public Library adjoins the Governor's Palace, and is one of the finest specimens of architecture in the town. The style of the whole edifice is grand and regular; and the arcade which extends along the whole length forms a delightful portico, and gives the facade a very imposing appearance. This structure was erected during the reign of the Grandmaster Rohan, but was not made use of as a library until the year 1811, when Sir H. Oakes, the British Governor, had all the books transported from their former incommodious lodging, near the Public Treasury, to their present situation.

The Public Library had its origin in the time of the Bailiff Ludovico Guerin de Tencin, who, endowed it with a great number of his own books, and procured for it vast legacies of literature from other sources. Not being able to make a sufficient provision, for its maintenance at his death, it was made over to the Order, and afterwards enriched by the private libraries of the Knights, who at their decease were obliged to bequeath all their books to this institution. The number of volumes now existing is about 40,000.

But this figure is on the increase owing to the continual addition of new works recommended by the active Librarian and the committee of the Library.

In such a collection, as one might expect from the manner in which it was brought together, there are many books of very little worth ; however, any person desirous of examining the records of antiquity, or of traversing the extensive fields of the scientifical research of by-gone days, or of deriving amusement from the peregrinations and voyages of the ancients, or of studying long treatises on military tactics and enginery, all the intermediate tastes from the most zealous disciple of Euclid, to the most pitiable novel reader,—may here find ample provision to satisfy his most enlarged desires. In fact, one may find almost any thing but a few *new* books.

The works in this Library are written principally in Latin, French and Italian; however, there is a small collection of English literature, and a few books in other European languages.

In the same room with the library is also kept a small collection of antiquities and curiosities, found at various times in this island and at Gozo, together with a few birds, a wolf, a wild cat and a snake all stuffed. The principal antiquities are the following:

Several Phœnician and other coins or medals which are not generally exposed, but kept under the care of the Librarian.

Several earthen jugs and lachrymatories, upon one of which certain Phœnician letters are perceivable although illegible.

A statue of Hercules of Parian marble in very good condition. The god is crowned with a garland of poplar, reclining on his club, and exhibiting a very calm and placid countenance.

The torso of a Diana in marble, found during the excavations recently undertaken for the extention of the Grand Harbour; the work is by a Grecian artist.

A square altar dedicated to Proserpine, on one of the sides of which two men are represented as offering a fish to the goddess; and on

another is the emblem by which the Syracu-
sans designed Sicily. It consists of a head
from which issue three legs, so disposed as to
form the three extremities of a triangle.

A Phœnician inscription on two pieces of
marble, which has been differently translated
by the several persons who have made the attempt; an undeniable proof that very little is
known in our days of the ancient Punic. These
monuments contain also a Greek inscription:
but the genuineness of both has been much
questioned.

A small brass figure, found at Gozo, representing a young beggar seated in a basket,
which is covered with large letters, as also is
the tippet which is thrown over his shoulders.
These letters appear to be a compound of Greek
and Gothic characters, and are very difficult to
decipher. An ingenuous writer thought he
discovered on it the figure of the cross, preced-
ed by the word OYΠEI for ETIYΠH which together he renders *Le Seigneur fut frappé.*

A small marble figure found at Gozo representing the wolf suckling Romulus and Re-
mus.

A marble slab containing two basso rilievo
figures representing Tullia and Claudia, the
former the daughter of Cicero, the latter the
wife of Cecilius Metellus; who both lived at
the same time. The inscriptions on this monument are very plain; one is TVLIOLA . M.

TVLII . F. and the other CLAVDIA. ME-
TELLI.

Another square marble stone containing a
bust in basso rilievo of Zenobia, wife of Ode-
nat, king 'of Palmyra. The inscription which
surrounds this figure is in good preservation;
it reads, ZENOBIA . ORIENTI . DOMINA ; and bears
the date AN . DNI . CCLXXVI.

A stone altar and other small idols found
in the course of the excavations at Hagiar-
Kim, representing the seven Brothers Kabiri
that figured in that Temple dedicated to As-
tarte.

Besides the above there are several other
Greek and Latin inscriptions, and very perfect,
and of little import.

This library is open to the public every day,
the principal feast-days excepted. Any person wishing to read here makes known to the
librarian what book he desires, and is then at
liberty to sit until the hour appointed for clos-
ing the room. It is also allowed to take any
books home, the time allowed for their reten-
tion being regulated according to the size of
the work.

The Garrison Library is in the building on the
left hand side cf the Main Guard on the Piazza
San Giorgio and consists at present at about
5000 volumes of English literature. There are
also a few works in French and Italian. Any
person wishing to subscribe is to write his name

in a book kept by the Secretary, which is submitted to the Committee for approval. The entrance money of all officers and gentlemen holding civil appointment is respectively to a sum equivalent to two days' pay as well civil as military the annual subscription of such 30s. sterling. No entrance money is required from private persons who may wish to subscribe. Temporary subscribers are obliged to pay the sum of 5s. monthly.

The great convenience in this institution are the newspapers and periodicals, of which it provides a good supply. These must remain on the Library table eight days before being put into circulation, during which time they are free to any subscriber who may wish to read them. For this purpose a Reading-room is provided, which is open nine hours a day in winter, and twelve in summer.

THEATRE ROYAL.

It was recently constructed on the site of the old Auberge d' Angleterre at the top of Strada Reale. The new Theatre is a noble edifice, of the Grecian order, and would have a just claim to elegance if it were lighter in its form and less profusely decorated in the exterior. Notwithstanding its defects, this building at the entrance, to the city, has a magnificent appearance, having a portico of the Corinthian order; and the interior is richly decorated, and

NEW OPERA HOUSE.

offers great accommodation in the boxes and pit. This work, commenced under che administration of Sir Gaspard Le Marchant, cost the Malta exchequer no less a sum than. £50,000. The saloon is remarkable for its elegance but leads tot he interior through low and narrow passages. The building, however, does not possess any accommodation for the painting of scenery, or any residence for actors, who, in the old Theatre, had their dwellings contiguous to it.

THEATRE MANOEL.

This was the public Theatre until the erection of the one just mentioned.

This building is situated in the street named after it *Strada Teatro*. It was erected by the Grandmaster Manoel Vilhena in the year 1731, and presented nothing remarkable in its exterior or interior construction ; but it was repaired in the year 1844 and since then is worthy of the attention of the traveller. Government grants the use of the Theatre gratis, and it is supplied in eight months of the year, October to May inclusive with italian operas and occasionally in the other four months June to September with an Italian prose company. Occasionally the Naval and the Military officers of the garrison as well as Maltese amateurs exhibit themselves as actors on the stage for the amusement of the public.

It will be allowed by all, that the intention of most players in acting is to procure money, and of the company in attending the theatre is to seek amusement. Hence it will be found here, as every where else, that the plays performed generally correspond with the taste of the audience.

CASTELLANIA.

In this public edifice up to a few years back were the Criminal Court, the Courts of the Magistrates of Judicial Police ; as also the office of the Executive Police; before their removal to the Auberge d' Auvergne in Strada Reale.—The principal portion of the building is now used as a secondary school for females, and the remaining portion has been let on lease to the Gas Company and other parties. It is situated in Strada Mercanti, and was rebuilt by the Grandmaster Emmanuel Pinto in the year 1758, as appears from an inscription over the entrance. In the same street opposite the Monte di Pietà, is the

BANCO DEI GIURATI.

In the time of the Order, the Office of the Magistracy for supplying the inhabitants with corn and other articles of food, and for fixing the market-prices was held in this building. This court consisted of four native Magistrates elected by the Grandmaster, and was presided over by a Bailiff Seneschal. Until the late abolition of the corn monopoly under the British government, the office of the Grain Department was held here. At present it is the Post Office.

MARKET.

A new market was built on the site of the old one, under the administration of Sir Gaspard Le Marchant, on the models of the *Halles* of Paris. It consists of a vast enclosure of stone, surmounted by an iron roof which is supported by several pillars of the same metal. The interior is occupied by rows of stalls for vendors, divided into passages. There are various pumps for the preservation of cleanliness which draw water from a large tank excavated under the foundation of this building. A ditch surrounds the market and gives admittance into the numerous stores constructed under this edifice.

QUARANTINE HARBOUR.

and Lazzaretto.

The gate called Marsamuscetto leads down a long flight of stairs, and over a drawbridge, to the shore of the Quarantine Harbour. Here is a large building, the upper part of which is occupied by the Health Office, and that of the Captain of the Ports; and the lower floor is divided into separate open apartments, where the captains of vessels in quarantine generally come with their boats in order to transact business with the people of the town. This is called the *Parlatorio* and each room is provided with two wooden rails in order to prevent the parties from coming in contact with each other.

Taking a boat we may cross over to visit the Lazaretto, accompanied by a *guardiano*, whose business it is to see that we do not infringe any of the sanitary laws. Before landing this person must demand permission of the Quarantine Office, and if there is no objection, we are at liberty to proceed and call upon any friend whom we may have undergoing his imprisonment in this establishment. Each division of the building is provided with a small room close to the shore, where persons are permitted to converse with each other, under the same restrictions as mentioned in the Parlatorio. The fixed regulation in regard to the payment of boats in this harbour frees the stranger from the annoyance he usually meets with from the boatmen in the other. The price is 6*d*. for each half hour.

On arriving in a vessel from a suspected port the traveller is invited by one of the officers of the establishment to land and visit the apartment were he is destined to pass his quarantine. In case he wishes to hire furniture over and above that provided by the Government, consisting of a table two chairs, and two bed-boards and trestles, he may do so from a person priviliged for the purpose, who, at a pretty high rate, will supply him with any thing he may require. In regard to food, should the person not possess the means of ordering a breakfast and dinner at the high rate charged by the *Trattoria* connected with the Lazaretto, he stands a good chance of suffering from hunger, unless he has friends in the town who will undertake to supply him ; because the only plan by which he may otherwise procure it, through caterers, is so badly regulated, as frequently to occasion the greatest inconvenience to travellers. As the guardiano placed over you is not allowed to serve in any way, (though you are obliged to pay him a salary, besides supplying him with food) one must almost necessarily hire a servant, who may charge as much as 2s. 3d. per day. In the latter case, however, the sum to be rewarded is according to agreement ; but as regards the guardiano, the price is fixed by the Government.

The day on which the passenger lands begins to count as the first of his term ; but should he neglect to open his trunks, &c. in order to air his baggage on this day, he runs the risk of being detained a day longer. The morning of the termination of his quurantine goes into the account as one day, and he is permitted at an early hour to leave for the city.

The chief part of the magazines and other

buildings of the Lazaretto were built by the
Grandmaster Lascaris, but have been lately
much improved by the British Government.
They occupy a site on a small island which is
joined to the mainland on the western side by
a stone bridge. Although lately, quarantine
may be said to have been totally suppressed,
communication with all countries being in free
pratique.

Quarantine is rigorously proclaimed against
visitations of cholera which gave constant proof
of its propagation by infection.   Science with
its positive and negative data as to the con-
tagious nature of the disease, is not yet authorized to suppress a sanitary measure on which
the safety of an entire country depends.

On the same island stands a strong bulwark
called

FORT MANOEL.

This fortress was erected by the Grandmaster Ant. Manoel de Vilhena, in the year 1726,
as appears from an inscription over the entrance
surmounted by a copper bust of the founder.
The walls of this fort are very strong, enclosing
a spacious yard, in which are three ranges of
buildings, each containing two rows of apartments, capable of lodging a garrison five hundred strong. Adjoining one of the above buildings is a small church, dedicated, to St. An-
thony of Padova, at present only used occasio-

nally by some clergyman who may happen to be in quarantine.

In the centre of the court was a bronze statue of the Grandmaster Vilhena, on a high square base, containing an elaborate eulogy, on its four sides, of the virtues and mighty deeds of the founder. The observation of Sig. D' Avalos in regard to this monument was worthy of notice. He suggests that it should be transplanted over to some conspicuous place in Valletta, in order to embellish the city; as, where it then stands, it was almost buried, and can neither be seen nor admired by the public.

The project of Sig. D' Avalos was carried out under the Government of Sir Gaspard Le Marchant, who caused that statue to be placed on the square of the Public Library. This square was, like those round St. John's Church, planted with trees and ornamented with a fountain and public *cafè*.

To the north-east of Fort Manoel, on the point called Cape Dragut, in memory of that famous corsair who was slain here during the great siege of Malta, stands another called

FORT TIGNE'

This fortress was erected in the year 1796, under the direction of the Commander Tousard and named after the Cavalier Tignè, the engineer who planned the design of the barracks of St. Elmo. This fort was built in order to act in junction with the castle of St. Elmo for the defence of the entrance into the quarantine harbour. Though small, it is very strongly fortified, and is extensively mined. The mines are cut out of the solid rock, and have two outlets: one by the side of the staircase which leads up to the fort, and the other, at some distance from it, near the beach on the north. On the top of the fort are four entrances leading down to the mines underneath, which separate in four directions according to the points of the compass. These passages are again separated into smaller divisions, containing apartments for the deposit of the powder destined to blow up the fort in case of its seizure by an enemy. It is at present garrisoned by a small body of artillery and a company of line.

TOUR ROUND THE WALLS OF VALLETTA.

Before taking leave of the City I would invite the stranger to a walk round the walls, especially those which overlook the ditch, where are several monuments raised to the memory of various deceased governors of the island, and other illustrious persons. Under the bastion of St. Michael lie the remains of Capt. Spencer, R. N. to whose memory a pillar was also erected on the heights of Corradino, in the Great Harbour. Below this was another monument, projected by the Maltese, to the memory of the late governor Sir F. C. Ponsomby. The expenses of this work were defrayed by public subscription. It was struck by lightning, and having been greatly damaged was subsequently demolished.

Under the Cavalier St. John, within a small grove of trees, is the tomb which encloses part of the remains of the Marquis of Hastings, who governed this island previous to the appointment of Sir F. C. Ponsomby. Beyond this is the New Barracca a kind of parterre where several other monuments are erected to the memory of noble personages, and where the ashes of the late Governor Sir Thomas Maitland repose in a secluded part.

The view from this place is very extensive and beautiful, and as it overlooks the great Harbour and its several creeks, with the sight of vessels of every size anchored therein,—the three towns which are directly opposite, the castles which defend the port, the Marina, the Floriana suburbs, and a great part of the country,—it forms one of the most pleasant and agreeable places of rest which the city affords.

A new Protestant Church has been erected on the western side of the Barracca.

On the walls of the town which defend the entrance of the Great Harbour is the Old Barracca, in which is planted a grove of trees surrounding a massy monument, raised to perpetuate the memory of Sir J. Ball, first British

Governor of the island. This also is a place of public concourse, enjoying a very pleasant view of the sea and of the harbour.

Having finished the tour of the most interesting localities in the city, we invite the stranger to a walk without the city gates, in the direction of the suburb called

FLORIANA.

This place is surrounded with strong fortifications planned and superintended by the engineer Col. P. P. Floriani, sent from Rome by the Pope, at the urgent request of the Grandmaster, in the year 1635. It is provided with four gates : one leading up from the beach called *della Marina*; two others opening in the direction of the country, one called *St. Ann's Gate*, and the other *Notre Dame Gate*; and a fourth enclosing the advanced works called *Des Bombes*.

These two gates, St. Anne's and Porte des Bombes, were lately remodelled on a better design, and divided into two openings, one for ingress, and the other for egress, rendering the passage of vehicles and foot-passengers more commodious.

On the outer front of the latter are to be seen the impress of several balls, which were fired by the Maltese when they blockaded the town against the French.

The open unoccupied space within these fortifications is divided by a long narrow enclosure, dignified with the title of the Botanical Garden. This is a place of public resort, and serves more as a pleasant walk than for the study of botany. There are however, a number of flowers collected here, and even a little green spot in Malta may be likened to an oasis in the desert.

Near the above is another garden, called *Argotti*, situated within the precincts of the walls which owes its improvements to the late General Villette. Though not quite so abundant in flowers as the former, it is much more extensive, contains more wood, and combines some of the beauties of native rural scenery with the embellishments of art; but lately it was much more improved as well as adorned with new plants and handsome fountains; it possesses a most charming view of the country beyond, and serves now for public resort and agreable walking.

HOUSE OF INDUSTRY.

This building, erected by the Grandmaster Manoel de Vilhena, was originally intended as a conservatory for poor girls, where they were taught to do a little work and in other respects to perform all the offices of nuns. In 1825 this establishment underwent an entire reform, and until very lately was in a very thriving condition as regards the occupation of its inmates. A great diversity of labour was done here, such as weaving, knitting' making lace, sewing, washing, shoe-making, straw-plaiting, cigar-making, and many other very useful branches of female manufacture. The girls, however, were never allowed to go out, unless under the conduct of the Lady Superior, and in this respect the establishment differed little from a nunnery. In case any application should be made for a servant, it was left to the option of some one chosen for the purpose, whether she would accept the situation. But the training which these girls received here was not at all calculated to fit them to be useful in household work. Another means by which they might be liberated was by marriage. A respectable young man desiring a wife, and holding acquaintance with any young woman in this establishment, might request her in marriage, and she was quite at liberty to leave, if she chose, for this purpose.

Since the breaking out of the cholera, which took place in the year 1837 and which necessitated the temporary dispersion of the inmates, this institution has not assumed its former system. A great number of the best workwomen left, and those who remained were only occupied in making clothes for themselves, and other labour connected directly with the establishment. One hour daily was set apart for teaching them to read and write.

But this building lately has been greatly improved and turned into a central hospital. It is formed of two stories and divided in two separate and large ranges of rooms, each one of them is to receive the male or female patients; it has also an adjoining wing for persons infested with venereal disease. The propriety of this place, the health of its site, the accomodations within and the regularity of the service render this establishment worthy of the notice of foreigners. The girls who were formerly in the house of industry were provisionally removed to the neighbouring asylum for the aged.

The lower part of the back side of this building forms a barrack for a regiment of the British garrison.

ASYLUM FOR THE AGED.

Descending a long staircase close by the Barracks, the traveller passes through a gate called *La Polverista*, which leads him to this establishment. It was erected by the same Grandmaster who founded the above mentioned institution, in the year 1734, and is now under the direction of the local government. Here are collected a great number of old and infirm persons, who are furnished with all necessaries of life, and provided for as long as they live. Each one is supplied with a bed, a trunk for his clothing, and a stool. The ringing of a bell calls them together for their meals; and it is a most interesting sight to see a long table lined with hoary heads sitting down to eat, apparently happy end comfortable in the last stage of their earthly existence. The aged females are kept separated from the males.

The open space before the building has lately been planted with trees and flowers, which makes it a very pleasant and agreeable walk. Following the pathway which leads from the Asylum, the traveller reaches the house and garden called

SA MAISON.

This is a delightful spot, containing a most charming view of the Quarantine harbour, the Pietà, and the country beyond. The garden, though small, is laid out with exquisite taste, and is well supplied with flowers and fruits. The battlement which encloses it on one side is almost covered with ivy; giving it at a distance a most beautiful appearance. This house belongs to Government.

Beneath the bastion, which extends along the Poor Asylum to this villa, is a very massy arch leading down to the shore of the Quarantine Harbour. The architecture of this piece of workmanship is very much admired by conoisseurs; the curve is of a tortuous and oblique form, and extends over a space of about thirty feet in width. It was thrown by the Maltese engineer Barbara, who assisted Colonel Floriani, in the erection of the fortifications which surround these suburbs.

PROTESTANT BURIAL GROUND.

A gate which bounds the precincts of the Poor Asylum leads down to this repose of the dead. Two extensive enclosures have already been filled up with the mortality of English residents, and a third, opened about ten years ago, is rapidly occupying its space with the bones of our countrymen. This latter is planted with flowers and trees, and contains many sumptuous monuments, the only seniority which the noble can now boast over the base, or the rich over the poor. Here repose many who sought in a foreign country a more genial climate for diseased nature, but whose destiny it was to be borne by strangers to their long home. Here they rest as quiet as in the sepulchre of their fathers, and will sleep on blendid with other dust, until the resurrection morn.

Let not the passer by neglect to receive the lesson which this place affords, and which is very simply inculcated on one of the tombs, in the following stanza:

Stop, traveller stop, ere you go by,
As you are now, so once was I;
As I am now, so you must be;
Prepare yourself to follow me.

The dilapidated tombs, the crumbling urns, and

M

weather-worn inscriptions, in the more ancient burial-grounds, prove what faithless remembrancers these are of recording to posterity our real excellencies ;—what a poor substitute for a set of memorable actions is polished alabaster or the mimicry of sculptured marble. The only way of immortalizing our characters, a way equally open to the meanest and most exalted fortune, is so to live as not to fear to die. Even the tongues of those, whose happiness we have endeavoured to promote, must soon be silent in the grave; but this virtue shall be inscribed indelibly on that book, from which the revolution of eternal ages shall never efface it.

Close by the English burial-grounds is one owned by the Greek church.

A new cemetery has lately been constructed outside the Porte des Bombes at the Pietà, in a place called *Ta Braxia*. It is divided into sections for the several religious creeds that wish to make use of it and is under the control of a Committee.

CAPUCHIN CONVENT.

This building, erected under the auspices of the Grandmaster Verdala, in the year 1584, is situated on a very interesting locality, commending an extensive view of the Great Harbour and of the country. The lower part of the edifice is occupied by the church of the convent, and a spacious court. The upper story is traversed by several narrow corridors lined with the cells of the monks, of which there are about sixty. The walls of the passages are covered with pictures, representing several miracles performed by the saint of this order. Over each cell is a small Latin inscription taken from the Holy Scriptures.

This convent is very much frequented on holidays, when a great number come here to while away an hour in traversing the corridors, examining the pictures which decorate the walls, reading the accounts of the mighty deeds of this brotherhood, chatting with some of the fraternity, or enjoying the fine air and beautiful prospect which surrounds the place.

The church contains nothing remarkable.

Below the church is an extensive vault called the *Carneria,* or Charnel-house, which is one of the most horrifying and disgusting spectacles I ever beheld. Here, those monks who die in the convent, are dressed in their clericals, and fixed up in niches until they fall to decay. The bones of such are taken and nailed upon the walls, in regular order, so as to form a kind of decoration; and the skulls are likewise arranged in rows along the ceiling. In one of the sides of this vault are two enclosed coffins, containing the bodies of two friars, who died in odour of sanctity.

CASA DELLA MADONNA DI MANRESA.

This building is situated opposite the New Central Hospital, and was erected in the year 1751 at the expense of D. Pietro Infante, Grand Prior of Crato in Portugal. It contains a small church of an oval form, which is one of the neatest houses of worship I have seen at Malta. The whole establishment is remarkable for the plainness and simplicity of its architecture; and at the same time, for its clean and decent appearance. It consists of several passages or corridors, on the walls of which are hung a vast variety of old paintings, arranged in symmetrical order, and lined on both sides with small rooms, each containing the most necessary articles of household furniture. In one angle of the building is a spacious yard, very tastefully laid out with flowers.

This institution was originally intended as a place of retreat for such persons as wished to perform the *Exercises of St. Ignatius*, consisting of meditations for ten successive days, during which time they secluded themselves from the rest of the world, and gave up all their temporal cares. At present it is used for the same purpose, by a portion of the clergy, during eight days by such as are about to present themselves for ordination. The three days of Carnival is another season when this establishment is sometimes crowded with the more religiously disposed from among the respectable classes of the people, who pass the time here in hearing masses, and sermons, confessing, meditation, and other devout duties.   Twice a year, also three days are appointed for such of the country people who desire to avail themselves of the quiet retirement and religious privileges which this place affords.   The establishment provides nothing but soup and lodging for any of the above ; so that all persons wishing to enjoy better fare must bring it along with them.

A spacious apartment in the building is set apart as the public refectory.   This is supplied with chairs and tables for the convenience of the inmates, who during their stay generally dine together.

A portion of this edifice was lately turned into a Seminary by the Archbishop, Mons. Pace Forno, for the superior instruction of the clergy.

Besides the above, there are two other churches in Floriana, one dedicated to St. Publius, recently widened after a bad taste of architecture, and the other called *dell'Immacolata Concezione di Maria*; which latter appartains to the Government.   It is generally known by the name of *Sarria*, so called after the Cavalier F. Martino de Sarria, who founded it in the year 1585. In consequence of a vow made during the time of the plague, it was repaired and enlarged by the Order in 1676, but contains nothing worth noticing; except some paintings by Mattias Preti. On the walls are hung many small pictures, placed there as the fulfillment of vows, representing the persons in their distress, and the real or imaginary cause of their deliverance.

The suburb of Floriana has increased in importance and in the number of its inhabitants. It is now a parish independent of that of *San Paolo* in Valletta, to which it was formerly attached. Many public sites having been sold by the government, numerous buildings were rapidly raised, and lately, after the demolition of the old Lunatic Asylum, a great many constructions were formed on its pleasant site, which commands a fine view of the whole extension of the Grand Harbour.

———

Having terminated the circuit of Floriana, I shall now pass over to observe what is most remarkable on the opposite side of the Great Harbour, including the three towns of Borgo, Burmola and Senglea.

This division of the island contains several small bays or creeks, formed by narrow peninsulas of land jutting out into the Great Harbour. On the two principal of these stand the cities of Borgo and Senglea, separated by a piece of water which runs inland as far as the centre of Burmola, and called formerly the Port of the Gallies. As the former of the above mentioned cities was the first residence of the Order we shall give it the precedence in the following description.

BORGO or CITTA' VITTORIOSA.

On the arrival of the Knights of St. John at Malta in 1530, this spot, which at that time was only occupied by a few huts, was selected as the place of their residence, and from that circumstance took the name of the *Burgh* or *Borgo*. After the victory gained over the Turks in 1565, (a short sketch of which I shall give at the end of the description of the three cities) it was dignified with the title of the *Città Vittoriosa*, or the *Victorious City*; in commemoration of which defeat, a statue of Victory was erected by the Grandmaster in the square of St. Lawrence, which exists to the present day. This city continued to be the seat of government until the year 1571, when the whole body of the Knights moved over to Valletta, which from that time became the conventual residence of the Order.

The site on which the small town of Borgo stands is very uneven, the streets are unpaved narrow and irregular, and consequently not remarkably clean. In general the houses are built much in the same manner with those of Valletta, but come far behind the latter in the neatness of their exterior, and the finish of their interior. Though there are several wealthy persons resident in the city it is chiefly inhabited by the second and third classes of the people, many of whom are engaged in the seafaring line.

The inner side of the peninsula is not walled in with fortifications these being rendered unnecessary by the castle of St. Angelo, and the forts of the Point and St. Michael, on the opposite town of Senglea. The outer side, however, towards the bay called *Calcara*, is defended by a strong wall which reaches the whole length of the city and encloses it by forming an angle at the termination of the above mentioned bay, and continues the line until it joins with the Harbour of the Gallies. That part of the bulwark which crosses the peninsula is defended by a deep ditch, which is traversed by a bridge leading into the city, and by the cavaliers of St. John and St. James which overlook the entrance. The chief defence of the city, as also of the Great Harbour, is the Castle of St. Angelo, which on account of its importance merits a more particular description.

CASTLE OF ST. ANGELO.

The first notice which we have of the occupation of this site for a place of defence is in the year 870, when the Arabs, after dispossessing the Greeks, erected here a small fort for the purpose of guarding their marauding vessels which anchored in the Great Harbour. On the arrival of the Knights of St. John it was made the chief bulwark of the town, aud consequently was very much enlarged. In 1686 new fortifications were added to it under the auspices of the Grandmaster Gregorio Carafa, and finally it assumed its present state in the year 1690, under the reign of Adrian de Wignacourt, as may be seen from an inscription on the outer gate.

On the site on which this castle stands, there was formerly the famous temple of Ianus, to which Cicero refers in his *Verrine;* it was a very rich temple until the time of the Roman domination, and was completely destroyed by the Arabs.

Towards the mouth of the Great Harbour this fort presents an imposing front, consisting of four batteries, built one above another in the style of an anphitheatre, mounting fifty-one guns beside those which are posted on the cavalier and the walls connected with it. The fort is separated from the town of Borgo by a ditch, into which the sea runs from the two harbours which flank it at both extremities. This ditch is about twenty-five yards in width, and according to tradition occupies the ancient site of the temple of the goddess Juno.

St. Angelo is at present garrisoned by a detachment of British artillery, under the command of a captain who occupies the building formerly tenanted by the Grandmaster. The only object of interest to be noticed within the walls is an extensive powder magazine, and a small Gothic chapel built on a level with the uppermost battery, and containing two sienite pillars which were probably brought by the Knights from the island of Rhodes.

VICTUALLING YARD.

A large extent of the inner wharf of Borgo is occupied by a range of magazines, with a covered portico, furnished with everything necessary for the supply of the British fleet. This place is called the Victualling Yard.

A little further from these buildings there were three long arched entrances, where the Gallies of the Knights were drawn up to undergo repairs, but they have lately been demolished, and in the room of them has been built a very beautiful edifice for the use of Her Majesty's Naval Bakery.

The row of buildings which line the mole above the magazines are at present occupied by the officers belonging to this naval establishment; they were formerly the residence of the Captain and Lieutenant General of the fleet of the Order, and of the Commanders of the gallies.

INQUISITOR'S PALACE.

This is an extensive building, situated in the street called *Strada della Porta Maggiore* and at present forms the mess-house for the officers of the British garrison stationed at the barracks of Fort St. Michael in Senglea. There is nothing particular to be noticed in the upper part of the edifice, and the passages which lead down to the cells underground, and which formed the prisonhouse of the poor wretches who unfortunately fell into the hands of this tribunal, have long since been walled up. About ten years ago, whilst digging to form a wine cellar, a rack was discovered in one of the subterraneous apartments.

The office of the Inquisition was introduced in the island of Malta by Pope Gregorio XIII in the year 1575, during the reign of John de La Cassiera. This circumstance took place on account of an action brought against the bishop of Malta by the Grandmaster, for interfering with the religious concerns of the Knights, which had ever been ruled and directed by a council of the Order. In order to decide to what lengths the bishop's jurisdiction should extend, Gregory agreed to send an Inquisitor to Malta, whose intervention, however, was not accepted until the Council of the Order had exacted a promise from the sovereign pontiff, that the officer sent from the court of Rome should never act but in conjunction with the

Grandmaster, the Bishop, the Prior of the church of St. John, and the Vice Chancellor of the Order; by which means the new tribunal was divided between the Inquisition and the principal officers of the state. But this prudent arrangement lasted a very short time. The Inquisitors, from a spirit of emulation so common among themselves, and on pretence of maintaining the authority of the Holy See, contrived to get fresh assessors ; and, in order to become absolute in their tribunal, endeavoured to establish a degree of domination in the island, and, frequently struggled hard to make it supersede the legitimate one. To effect this purpose, they pursued the following method : any Maltese who was desirous of throwing off the authority of the Order might address himself to the office of the Inquisition, which immediately presented him with a brief of independence, to which was given the name of *patent*: Those who took out the patent were called the *Patentees of the Inquisition;* which implied, that in consequence of the said patent, they and all their family were under the immediate protection of the Holy See; so that in all causes, either civil or criminal, the patentee was first tried in Malta by the tribunal of the Inquisition, and, if the condemned party thought proper to make a last appeal to the Court of Rome, he was there tried a second time by a tribunal called *La Rota.* Whilst the trial lasted, their persons were secure, and the government of the Order could neither commit them to prison, nor punish them in any manner whatsoever.

During the reign of la Cassiera the Inquisition had carried its designs to such a pitch, that three of the holy brotherhood were seized for forming a plan, in conjunction with some Spanish knights, to murder the Grandmaster. In 1657, fourteen years after the establishment of the tribunal, the Grand Inquisitor Odi raised disturbances by his interference in the election of a Grandmaster; and in 1711 one named Delci carried his pretensions to the highest degree of arrogance. He began by insolently demanding that the carriage of the Grandmaster should stop on meeting his; and afterwards insisted that the infirmary belonging to the Order should for the future be under his jurisdiction.

This hospital, which had ever been regarded as the most privileged spot on the island, and into which even the Marshal of the Order could not enter within leaving his truncheon at the door, was entrusted to the care of some French Knights, who were particularly zealous for their liberties, and who acknowledged no superior authority, but that of the Grand Hospitaller, who alone was permitted free entrance without leaving behind him the ensigns of his dignity; yet even here the officers of the Inquisition had the audacity to enter by surprise,

N

and to begin their visits of examination. But the moment the Overseer of the infirmary was informed of their conduct, he obliged them to depart immediately, and declared null and void all their proceedings. The Inquisitor Delci did not stop here; but without the smallest attention to the rights of the sovereign, and to prove his own superiority, distributed a great number of patents, such as we have already mentioned declaring in the most absolute terms, that every Maltese to whom they were granted became from that moment exempt from all obedience to the legitimate sovereign (*).

This tribunal continued its proceedings until the arrival of the French, who expelled them from the island, and confiscated all their property.

CHURCHES AND MONASTERIES OF BORGO.

St. Domenic's Convent.

Opposite the Inquisitor's Palace is a convent dedicated to St. Domenic, which is at present occupied by a few friars of the same order. The upper division of the building consists of several passages, containing the cells of the monks; but the whole is in a very delapidated condi-

(*) See Boisgelin, vol. II p. 140, 195, 220 ; and Vertot, tom. iv, p. 225 e seq.

tion, and unless repaired will soon fall to ruin. The church connected with the convent might once have made some pretence to elegance, but at present it has the appearance of being the worse for wear.

Church of St. Lawrence.

This is the parish-church of the città Vitto-riosa, and during the residence of the Order in this city, was made use of by them as their place of public worship. It contains several commodious chapels, and is rather richly ornamented. On one side stands an image of St. Lawrence, holding a large silver gridiron in his hand. This article was presented to the church by a Maltese, on the Anniversary of the feast of the saint, in fulfilment of a vow made by him during the prevalence of the cholera. The gridiron is about one yard and a half long and three quarters wide. The cost was 890 scudi, or 66*l*. 13*s*. 4*d*.

The large painting over the high altar of this Church, representing the Martyrdom of Saint Lawrence, an excellent work of Matthias Preti, well deserves the attention of visitors. This church contains several interesting and curious articles of sacred vestments brought by the Knights from Rhodes.

Santa Maria dei Greci.

This was formerly one of the chapels which belonged to the Greeks who followed the

Knights of St. John from Rhodes. The number
of this persuasion having greatly diminished,
this chapel was granted to the *Fratelli* (*) of
St. Joseph, who have it in their possession at
the present day. The only object of interest
worth noticing here is the sword and hat,
which the Grandmaster La Vallette wore, on
the day in which he drove the Turks from the
island. They are preserved in a glass case,
with the following inscription engraved on a
marble slab underneath:

Emmanuel Rohanus
Magnus Ordinis Hieros, Magister
Sacellum Deiparae Virgini
Consumatrice sacrum
Vetustate conlapsum
Cum omni cultu
Restuit anno MDCCLXXIX
Idemque providentia sua cavit
ut injuria superiorum temporum neglecta
decentiore loco servarentur
Ensis et Galerus
quae Joannes Valletta
ejusdem ordinis Supremus Magister
anno MDLXV
Turcis devictis
Melitae obsidione soluta
Republica bene gesta servantaque
lubens et laetus

(*). For the signification of this term see note pag. 108.

Heic sospes Dei genetrici
suspenderat.

Convent of Sta. Scolastica.

During the time of the Bishop Gargallo, the nuns composing this siterhood were transported from the Città Notabile, their original residence, to the present Convent which had formerly belonged to the Ursuline nuns of the Order of St. John. This was considered so great an innovation by the citizens of the Notabile, that the Commander Lascaris, afterwards Grandmaster, was sent to escort them in safety, lest they should be seized by the fury of the people.

The convent is large, and has a very neat church connected with it. On either side of the altar is a grated window, where the nuns are permitted to come, in order to hear mass. In one of these there is a small opening, from which they receive the Holy Communion.

BIRMULA or CITTA' COSPICUA.

This city lies inland between Borgo and Senglea, and is surrounded with a strong bulwark, which commences at the counter scarp of the former, and joins on with the walls of the latter, where they overlook the inner harbour called the Port of the French. This fortification was commenced in the year 1638, during the reign of the Grandmaster Lascaris, under the superintendence of the engineer Vincenzo Maculano, a Domenican friar sent over by the Pope for the purpose. The design of the defence was much enlarged under the Grandmaster Perellos, and was finally completed by Manoel de Vilhena in 1730.

On the hill, called Sta. Margarita which is situated just without the chief entrance of the Città Vittoriosa, is a nunnery dedicated to that saint, and also a conservatory for girls, under the direction of the Bishop of Malta. At the foot of the hill is a monastery of Carmelite monks, dedicated to St. Teresa. The parish church called *della Concezione* is a spacious building, but contains little worthy the attention of the traveller.

The chief part of the town of Birmula is situated on a low site, and is very thickly populated. The streets are generally narrow and irregular, and a great proportion of the houses, especially those situated near the walls, are nothing better than hovels. In this quarter, the city presents a very miserable appearance, not only from the mean aspect of the dwellings, but from the great accumulation of stones and rubbish which crowd the fortifications. One side of the wharf of the small harbour of Birmula is occupied by the old dockyard and naval arsenal, provided with every thing requisite for the supply of the British fleet in the Mediterranean. Part of the opposite shore is also taken up with magazines, destined for the same purpose.

The extreme southern point of the Birmula fortifications is defended by the Fort St. Francesco di Paola, garrisoned at present by a detachment of English infantry.

THE NEW DOCK YARD.

This magnificent ornament was for a very long time designed by the Order of St. John; in fact during the reing of the Grandmaster Rohan its construction was commenced in the Harbour of the French, but on account of some unforseen difficulties its continuation was suspended.

In the year 1815 the British Government meditated likewise such a work at a short distance from the site on which the present exists; but as after some years of labour and considerable expense, the rock had been found porous and full of cracks, it was also given up.

The site for the construction of this splendid addition to the port of Malta was made by cutting off the inner extremity of the harbour of the Gallies precisely opposite the market of Birmula. On each side around the dock are seen new buildings, suitable for manufacturing and repairing steam-engines and other naval articles as also coal wharfs &c. and thus they include all stores of different Naval departments.

The foundation of the work was laid in 1841; and the first pile was driven in the spring of 1843, under the superintendence of Rear Admiral Sir John Lewis. The first stone of the wall of the bason was laid on the 1st of May 1843, at a depth of 43 feet and 6 inches below the level of the sea; and the first stone of the Dock-Yard was solemnly laid by H. E. the Governor Sir Patrick Stuart on the 28th of June, 1844 occurring the anniversary of her most gracious majesty Queen Victoria's coronation. The ceremony was attended by the èclat that so important an occasion merited. The dock was opened also by the late Governor under the superintendence of Rear Admiral Sir Lucius Curtis; but the first vessel which entered its gates for the purpose of being overhauled was H. M's. Steamer *Antelope* under the Rear Admiral Superintendent Edward Harvey; the *Antelope* was received in the dock on Saturday the 5th of September, 1848. Thus Sir John Lewis had the honor of commencing this splendid ornament : Sir L. Curtis had the principal share in directing its continuation ; and Rear Admiral Edw. Harvey had the honor of first rendering it practically useful.

The following account of its dimensions, and the persons who have been principally engaged in planning and directing the construction of its different parts, will we believe, be found tolerably correct :

Whole length from entrance to the head 310 feet,
Length of the floor inside   —   — 230 ,,
Width at level of Coping   —   — 82 ,,
Depth of water in dock   —   — 25 ,,
Depth of water upon the apron—   — 23 ,,

The plan of the dock was the result of an inspection by Capt. Bradreth, R. E. Director of Works to the Lords of the Admiralty. The plan and working drawing were furnished by W. Scamp Esq. to whom is also due in a great measure, the honor of the execution of this noble and useful work. The works were carried on by M. Walter Elliot from 1845 to May 1847, when the dock itself was completed. The Caisson was built in England, and fitted up in Malta; and the removal of the Coffer Dam, as well as the immediate charge of the works in connection with the dock, were in the skilful hands of Mr. John Scott Tucker, late Admiralty Engineer at Bermuda.

The estimated cost of the dock, as laid before Parliament, was £ 45,000; it has however cost £ 60,000; the caisson costs about £ 3,000, and the factory buildings £ 40,000. What immense benefit to the island the expenditure of the principal part of this enormous sum in wages and materials has been ! It is useless for us to describe ; but we consider this to have been but a trifling part of the advantage. The presence of so many able Engineers and foremen has been, we doubt not, of considerable service to the native workmen, and many of them will have the occasion to look back with satisfaction and gratitude to the day when they first began to contribute their portion to this splendid monument of British liberality.

We congratulate the Mother Country on the completion of her magnificent work and our Island on its acquisition of this proof of British affection. It is indeed a work fraught with much importance to England as the first maritime power, and will, in a mercantile point of view, prove no less beneficial to the inhabitants of this Island.

A few years after the dock was completed, it was not found sufficiently large to admit large steamers, and it was therefore found necessary to extend it to the whole length of the old market of Cospicua, these new works were solemnly inaugurated on the return of Admiral Lord Lyons with the fleet from the Crimea.

Another more extensive Dock is now annexed to the former one, its entrance being from the French Creek, which is exclusively occupied by the Admiralty.

Following the road leading north from the above mentioned fort, we arrive at the outskirts of the city of Senglea.

SENGLEA OR ISOLA.

This city is situated upon the peninsula opposite Borgo, having the Harbour of the Gallies on one side, and that of the French on the other. Towards the former it is not walled in, but a strong bastion extends the whole length of the town towards the latter and then crosses the peninsula at the entrance of the principal gate, forming an exact counterpart to the fortifications on the opposite side: so that a line run across the extremities of the Galley Port would connect the walls of both cities. The chief defence of Senglea is the strong fortress of St. Michael which commands the entrance into the town, as well as the two harbours by which it is flanked. This fort was erected in the year 1552 by the Grandmaster John D'Omedes; the walls and other fortifications were raised in the subsequent reign by Claude de la Sengle, from whom the city took its name. Previous to this was called *Chersoneso,* and after the siege of 1565 was known by the name of *Isola* or the *Città Invitta.*

On the mole of the inner harbour was the *Merchant's Yard,* where all Maltese vessels and boats were built; on the outer, towards the end, is a large building, formerly appropriated to the Captains of the gallies, but now being improved, is occupied by several officers of the Dock Yard Department. This wharf is known by the name of *La Sirena*, (the Syren) from the circumstance that a figure of this creature formerly stood over the entrance into a small cave, at the commencement of the mole, to which the natives were accustomed anciently to resort as a place of amusement.

Senglea is in every respect superior to Borgo and Birmula. It contains many well built houses, and the streets are in general tolerably good, though none of them are paved. It includes one large church and a monastery : the former dedicated to the *Nativity of the Virgin Mary*, and the latter to St. Philip. On the wall just inside the entrance of the church is a marble slab, containing an inscription, put up to record the fidelity of the inhabitants during the siege, and obstinate refusal to accept the offered bribes from the Turks in order that they should desert the Order ; for which gallant action they were freed from the annual tribute, which they previously paid to the knights. The writing is as follows.

D. O. M.
Amplis. Hier. Ordini,
Principi Munificentissimo,
Fidei, et Bellicae virtutis remuneratori

*ob liberatum populum ab onere census
decreto sacri concilii status
edito, Magistero vacante,
IX Februarii MDC. ab incarnato Christo
Senglea Civitas Invicta
Grati animi monumentum p.*

On the wharf of the Sirena is a small establishment, founded in the year 1794 by Nicola Dingli and Maria Cornelia, two wealthy Maltese, for the reception of female convalescents belonging to this city and the village siggieui, who are received and lodged here for eight days after they leave the Public Hospital. There is a small chapel connected with this institution.

COTTONERA FORTIFICATIONS.

This vast bulwark, extending for several miles from the city Vittoriosa round the whole of Birmula with the *Firenzuola* fortifications, and joining the bastion of Senglea, was built in the year 1670 by the Grandmaster Nicholas Cotoner, and originally intended as a safe retreat for the whole population of the country in case of a siege. The fort of St. Salvador, erected by the Grandmaster Manoel de Vilhena, occupies an elevated position on the Cottonera lines about a mile to the east of Vittoriosa, and completely commands that city. In case of attack, this situation would be very dangerous in the hands of an enemy.

Within these vast lines of fortifications the Verdala Fortress has been constructed in the form of a citadel, and is now garrisoned by a regiment of the Line. Extensive tanks were also excavated under the administration of Sir H. Bouverie and Sir G. Le Marchant.

CAPUCHIN CONVENT.

Without the gate of St. Salvador, situated in a very pleasant and elevated spot, stands the above convent, built under the auspices of the Grandmaster Manoel de Vilhena. The only worth noticing in the church is a small chapel, built after the model of the *House of Loreto*.

NAVAL HOSPITAL.

The hill upon which this building is erected is known by the name of *Bighi*, so called after a Prior of the same name, who built a residence for himself on the present site of the Hospital. It is situated on a small piece of land, jutting out between the bay called *Renella* and that of *Calcara*. Until within the last five years, when the Naval Hospital was removed to this spot, it occupied a building within the walls of Vittoriosa. The present establishment is well worth the traveller's attention. The edifice is neat and extensive, and every thing requisite for the comfort of the patients is amply provided. A wide space of ground is walled in round the building, and is planted with shrubs and trees, forming a delightful walk for such as are convalescent.

FORT RICASOLI.

This fort was founded in the year 1670 by the Cavalier Gianfrancesco Ricasoli, who contributed the sum of £ 3000 towards defraying the expenses of the building, and endowed it with a large portion of his income. The Grandmaster Cottoner publicly acknowledged his gratitude to the knight for so generous an action, and ordered that it should be called after his name, Ricasoli. This fortress is built on the extreme point of an angular projection, and corresponds with St. Elmo on the opposite shore. The two forts together command the entrance into the Great Harbour. In itself it is a place of considerable strength, and is additionally guarded by the bulwarks which extend and ramify towards the Cottonera lines. From the sea, this fort, if tolerably garrisoned, would be quite impregnable. From the land side it could only be reached by surmounting a long succession of strongly defended posts, at each of which the assailants would be subject to imminent, almost insuperable danger.

On the 3rd of April 1807, this fort was the scene of an event, which as it is but little known, may be worth recording. During the progress of the war, when the necessity of large military supplies was hardly satisfied by the resources of our country, the expedient was adopted by our Government of entering into a commercial contract with different speculators, who engaged, for a certain remuneration, to levy troops, according to the emergency, from the peasantry of different countries, to be rendered disposable for foreign service when that service did not seem to require more trustworthy or veteran troops. A French noble proposed to raise for the Mediterranean service a regiment composed entirely of Greeks. The bargain being struck, he proceeded to gather together from the Levant, Archipelago and the Continent, a horde of various men, Greeks, Albanians, Sclavonians and what not, who were to be enrolled under the English banners, with the title of *Froberg's Regiment.* In a short time they were equipped, transported to Malta, and appointed to occupy this fort. The officers who had been placed over them were chiefly Germans; and in order to perfect them more, an English drill-serjeant or two, with an officer, were appointed to the same duty, and some artillerymen as usual remained in the garrison to superintend the guns. The severity exercised over the Frobergs by their commanders was increasingly aggraved, when they found that all the spacious promises of professional dignity, with which they had been lured into the service, were vain and delusive. A frequent use of bodily punishment, often inflicted by caprice, ripened these soldiers for rebellion, and the occasion of an officer striking a drummer on the face with a cane was the signal for open revolt. Several officers were killed by the rebels, and finally they closed the gates against the garrison of Valletta and declared themselves independant.

In their stronghold, these rebels bid defiance to the numerous troops that were at that time stationed in the garrison, and the dubious measures of the military governor Villetes, then second in command, so far assisted them, as to leave nothing to be dreaded but the consequence of blockade, which was established forthwith. An English artillery-officer and several of his men, who were still imprisoned within the fort, were obliged to assist in pointing the guns, and firing over shot into the city.

The scarcity of provisions and the absence of all subordination among the revolters, soon produced intestine quarrels, which, as might be expected in such a company, soon terminated in bloodshed. This state of things did not continue long; a large section burst open the gates, threw themselves in the midst of the English troops, leaving behind about one hundred and fifty of their companions in possession of the fort.

These resolute fellows still continued to man the walls, and to keep up their former hostile proceedings. Their affairs, however, were soon

rendered desperate.   An English Naval Officer,
named Capt. Collins, offered to take upon himself the capture of the fort; and accordingly
succeeded in storming it by night, and in secur-
ing all the men, with the exception of six, who
took possession of the powder-magazine, and
there defied the courage of the assailants, by pro-
testing that they would blow it up in case they
preserved in their endeavours to seize them.

Of the number taken, ten were hung and fifteen
musketted, on the plain of Floriana. Their execution, however, was carried on in the most inhuman
and barbarous manner. Pinioned and handcuffed
they were made to kneel upon their coffins without being blindfolded, and after the first volley
fired at them, several, still clinging to life, rose
up and ran about the plain pursued by the soldiers like so many hares. One in particular made
great efforts to escape; after stumbling close by
a well into which he had attempted to throw
himself, he managed to reach the bastions, from
which he cast himself headlong the height of one
hundred and fifty feet.   The soldiers in pursuit
followed him to the place of his fall, were finding that he still lived, they soon put an end to
his miserable existence.

But to return to the six rebels, who continued in possession of the powder magazine.
Confident of making advantageous terms with
the Governor, they persisted in their obstinate
resistance, and made no advances towards a

surrender. From time to time some one presented himself in order to negotiate with the besiegers, but to no avail ; nothing but an unconditional surrender would be listened to by the commandant. Five days passed away in this manner, during which time, all their urgent entreaties for provisions were obstinately refused, and the unfortunate wretches were reduced to a most pitiable condition. On the sixth these entreaties were pressed with additional importunities, and seconded with the threat, that in case of a refusal, or the non-assurance of pardon, they would blow up the fort as soon as the first vesper-bell tolled from St. John's cathedral. No notice was taken of this desperate menace, or any thought entertained that these six men valued life so little as to join together in so horrible a design for their own destruction. All was still until the appointed hour, when the fatal crash was heard, the stones of the magazine were seen rising in the air, and the whole building, with a part of the fortificacation, was reduced to ruins. The loss sustained by the besiegers from this explosion was considerable.

Some time had already elapsed, and the affair of the rebels had ceased to be talked of, when a priest returning home on a donkey, from a rather solitary quarter in the direction of the fort, was assailed by a man dressed in the Froberg uniform, who pointed his musket at him over a wall, and apparently intended to make him the receptacle for its contents. The affrighted father immediately took to his heels, and upon his arrival at home made known the circumstance to the police. An armed body was forthwith sent in pursuit of the bandit, which suceeded in discovering the retreat of the six poor wretches, whom it was imagined had been blown up with the magazine. Pale and emaciated they were secured with ease, and let into the town, and soon afterwards received the full reward of their inhuman deeds by a public execution.

From their own account of their escape, it appears, that during the siege they had continued to carry out one of the mines to the precints of the fortifications, leaving but a slender wall to abstruct their retreat, which they might throw down in a moment, during the night, without any noise, when they wished to escape. Until this work was completed, they continued to make every appearance of holding out, but when all was ready, a train of powder was laid at sufficient distance to secure them from the effects of the explosion, and which they kindled at the precise time of their threat. It seems to have been the hope of the rebels, that in getting free from the fort, they might fall in with some vessels on the coast, and thus make their escape from the island. If afterwards appeared, that they had actually attempted to seize a small boat, upon which occasion they narrowly escaped from being apprehended.

Later, this fort was the scene of another catastrophe. At the appearance of the Cholera in the year 1837, the inmates of the Poor-House and Hospital of Incurables, amongst whom a few cases of the fell disease had manifested themselves, were removed to this fort, with the view of entirely separating them from the population; but almost all those most unfortunate beings were mown down by death in the brief period of a few days. The place offered a most horrible spectacle.

On the bastion nearer the sea a Lighthouse has been constructed to point out to mariners the dangers attending the entrance into the Grand Harbour from that part.

SIEGE OF BORGO AND SENGLEA.

As I have had occasion during the foregoing description to revert several times to the siege of 1565, in which the above two cities were invested for upwards of two months, I shall proceed to give a short account of that event, in order that by the associations of history, an increased interest may be felt in examining the localities with which they are connected.

After the capture of St. Elmo by the Turks, which I have already noticed in my description of that fort, a christian slave was sent from the

Turkish camp to St. Angelo, in order to propose a negotiation; but being sent back with an answer of defiance, the entire peninsulas of the Bourgh and La Sengle were invested without delay. The latter town, and its principal defence, fort St. Michael, were the points against which the besiegers directed their fire. Several batteries, planted on Mount Sceberras and the hill of Corradin, completely commanded these posts, and as they were esteemed the weakest, the flower of the Order undertook their defence. The harbour of the French alone remained open, and here the Ottoman leader determined to make his principal assault; but as it was impossible for a flotilla to pass under the batteries of St. Angelo without certain destruction he determined to adopt the expedient of transporting a number of boats from Marsamuscetto into the Great Harbour, across the isthmus which joins Mount Sceberras to the mainland. The desertion of a Greek officer from his service, however, put the knights in timely possession of this project, and occasioned it to be materially altered.

Thus forewarned, the Grandmaster prepared to defeat the contemplated assault. The seaward walls of La Sengle were heightened by his orders, and the cannon on them brought to command the inner port at every point; while a vast stockade, extending from Mount Corradino to the point of Senglea was formed, by driving huge piles into the shallow water, and then fixing a chain on the top of them by means of iron rings. In order to remove this barrier, Mustapha dispatched a band of expert swimmers under the cloud of night, with axes in their girdles, to open a passage through the booms and palisades; but the noise of these adventurers alarmed the garrison, and the guns on the walls immediately commenced a fierce cannonade. Being too elevated, they threw their shot over the heads of the Turks, and therefore proved ineffective; but at the suggestion of Admiral de Monte, a party of Maltese swimmers were dispatched against them, and, after a sanguinary combat in the water, completely routed the Turks. A subsequent attempt was made to destroy the booms, and stakes, by means of cables worked on the shore by ships capstans; but this also was baffled by the intrepidity of the marines, who swam out again and cut the ropes.

Enraged at being thus circumvented in a favourite project, the Pasha, on the 5th of July ordered his guns to open simultaneously on the two towns. Accordingly, the vast batteries which had been raised on the hill of Sta. Margarita and the rock of Corradino commenced a furious cannonade against Fort St. Michael, and the bulwark of Senglea, while those on Mount Sceberras and the hill of Salvador played on Borgo and the castle of St. Angelo. The

cannonade did not cease until considerable
breaches were made in the advanced works of
both towns, and the Pasha was only delayed
from making an attempt to storm the latter,
from a desire that the Viceroy of Algiers would
soon arrive with a reinforcement to share in the
assault.

Hassan, the leader of the algerine troops,
soon came, accompanied by two thousand five
hundred chosen soldiers. He was the son of
the famous Barbarossa, and the son-in-law of
the scarcely less famous Dragut, who lost his
life on the cape on which Fort Tignè stands.
To this young warrior was committed, at his
own request, the land attack on Fort St. Michael, and to Candelissa his lieutenant, the maritime part of the enterprise. Under his superintendence, and in accordance with the Pasha's
original project, a number of boats were dragged overland from Marsamuscetto and launched
in the Great Harbour, where they were manned
with four thousand Algerine and Turkish soldiers. Under a galling fire of round shot and
musketry, the enemy sprang bravely upon the
stockade, which obstructed the entrance of his
fleet into the French Harbour, and with ham-
mers and hatchets endeavoured to demolish it.
After several attempts they succeeded in forming a passage to an uncovered part of the
beach at the extremity of Senglea. This head-
land was defended by a battery of six guns,

playing level with the water, and by a strong intrenchment, within which were posted a number of expert harquebusiers. Several discharges of shot among the assailants greatly diminished their numbers; but rendered desperate by the perils which surrounded them, after a combat of five hours, they forced the defenders to retire, and planted seven Turkish ensigns on the summit of the intrenchment.

The sight of the Moslem standard floating triumphantly on this outwork,filled the knights with shame and indignation, and a fresh body of them, headed by Admiral De Monte, renewed the battle. After a severe conflict, the Turkish pennons were torn down, and their defenders driven headlong from the rampart. All those who failed to reach the boats were sacrificed,many were shot while swimming after their boats, and of the boats themselves many were sunk by the fire of the batteries.

The landward attack, headed by the Algerine Viceroy in person, was not more successful. At the sound of a signal gun, his troops rushed gallantly towards the breaches on the side of the Birmula Gate and the castle of St. Michael and in a short space, a small corps of Algerines displayed their ensigns on several points of the parapet. A murderous discharge, however from the cannon of the fort poured death into the heart of the enemy, and drove them back again with great slaughter. Unable to stand

o

the steady and destructive fire of the knights,
the Viceroy at length sounded a retreat, leaving
flowers of his troops lifeless at the foot of
rampart.

he Turkish general did not fail to follow up
bloody effort with a fresh attack, but was
again as violently repulsed by the bravery of
the knights. Undismayed, however, by these
successive repulses, he ordered a kind of bridge
to be constructed by means of which he anti-
cipated his troops would be able to enter the
works. The Grandmaster, who regarded this
contrivance with apprehension, made two attempts to burn it by night; but the sleepless
vigilance of the enemy rendered them futile.
He at length determined to make a final attempt to destroy it by day, and his nephew,
Henry de La Vallette, was intrusted with the
perilous duty. At the head of a body of picked
men, and in the teeth of a heavy fire from the
Turks, he sallied out, accompanied by a brother
knight, with the intention of fastening a number of strong ropes to the principal posts and
beams of the bridge, so as to enable them to
drag it by main force from its position. The
design, however, was baffled by the fierce fire
of the arquebusiers, and the followers of young
La Vallette bore back the lifeless remains of
their leader into the fortress.

The Grandmaster, though secretly mourning
the fate of his nephew, did not allow himself to

be deterred for a moment from effecting his purpose. By his orders, an entrance was opened in the wall, immediately facing the bridge, through which a piece of artillery was brought to play on the whole structure. A few dischargers shattered it in such a manner as to render it unserviceable; and on the following night, it was set on fire and consumed to ashes.

Disconcerted by this event, the Pasha again ordered the Turkish batteries to open upon the two towns with redoubled activity, and the contest waxed daily more bloody and desperate. For four successive days the Christians were engaged in incessant skirmishes on the walls of La Sengle; and at length on the 2nd of August, the Turkish horns sounded an escalade. The Turks fought with extraordinary obstinacy; but at the end of six hours their ardour abated, and they retired from the breaches leaving them chocked with their dead. Five days afterwards, simultaneous attacks were made on Fort St. Michael and the bastion of Castile. The Janissaries, who led the van of the battle, advanced against the former fortress with warlike shouts, and though the ground over which they crossed was strewn with mutilated bodies, they fought their way to the top of the breach, and for four hours maintained their position. At this crisis, not only the knights, but the citizens, men, women and children, hovered on the skirts of the combat and supplied their

protectors with refreshments or flung missiles
and fire-works into the Ottoman ranks. Wearied and oppressed with fatigue the Christians
prepared for the worst, when suddenly, to their
astonishment and joy, they heard a recall
sounded along the Turkish line.   This season-
able relief was occasioned by a diversion on the
part of the Governor of the Città Notabile, who
observing from his post the cloud of smoke
which enveloped Fort St. Michael, hastily ordered a few squadrons of cavalry to make an attack on the nearest point of the Turkish position. The knights who commanded this detachment led it down to the Marsa, and massacred
all the sick and wounded which were found in
the hospital of the enemy.   The fugitives who
had escaped carried the news, that the Sicilian
succours had arrived, which caused Mustapha,
at the moment of victory to relinquish the
breach, and to march against this new foe.
His indignation knew no bounds when he discovered the true state of the case ; and had it
not been of the harassed condition of his soldiers and the entreaties of his officers, he
would have immediately marched back to the
field.

More than a fortnight elapsed before a new
attempt was made.   On the 18th of August,
the patience of the Turkish leaders became
quite exhausted ; and they once more made an
attack on the castle of St. Michael, with the

resolution of continuing it day and night until the towns were taken. A previous cannonade had almost rased a part of the walls of St. Michael; but it was in vain that the enemy endeavoured to break through the barriers which the besieged formed with their bodies. The assault was suspended for some time, and was again renewed after sun-set; but the assailants, disheartened by their frequent repulses soon gave up the attempt for the night.

August the 19th the assault was renewed with undiminished resolution, and continued on the 20th but with little success on the part of the enemy, though at a great expense of life on the side of the besieged.

The garrison had by this time become greatly diminished, the walls were mined in every direction, many of the outworks were in the hands of the Turks and the Knights advised the Grandmaster to blow them up and to retire into the fortress of St. Angelo. But La Vallette sternly rejected this counsel, and determined to keep his ground to the last.

No fresh assault was made until the 1st. of September, when the Janissaries endeavoured again to take possession of the breach; but their adversaries, and after a dreadful carnage they were obliged to retire from the conflict. At this crisis, when the battle was almost won by the valour of the knights, the long expected succours arrived from Sicily. The forces as-

sembled were two hundred knights, and about
eight thousand veteran troops, who disembark-
ed on the morning of the 7th of September,
in the bay of Melleha, together with their arms
and military stores. As soon as this expedition was landed, the Viceroy set sail and returned back to Sicily.

Though warned of the arrival of this reinforcement, the Turks imagined that nothing more
would be tried than to force the entrance of the
Great Harbour. Under this impression, they
blocked the entrance with stakes and booms,
and held themselves in readiness to defend the
barrier. Their consternation, consequently, was
extreme, when their scouts announced that a
Christian army had actually landed, and was in
full march against their camp. Rumour mag-
nified the Sicilian troops into an overwhelm-
ing force, and without waiting to ascertain
their real force, the Turkish general instantly
drew his garrison out of Fort St. Elmo, abandoned all his heavy ordnance, and hurried on
board his fleet. Scarcely, however, had he
accomplished this sudden movement, than he
obtained authentic information as to the number of his new enemies, and filled with shame,
he ordered his army to be relanded. But in a
few hours the labour of months had been rendered futile. The Maltese had already levelled
his lines and entrenchments, and the standard
of St. John once more waved over the cavalier

of St. Elmo. A few skirmishes took place in the interior between the two parties; but the last efforts of the Turkish leaders to retrieve a long series of reverses were ineffectual. On the same day the whole army embarked, and immediately weighed anchor for Constantinople.

Thus ended this memorable siege, in which 25,000 Turkish soldiers perished. On the other side, the loss was also great, amounting to between seven and eight thousand citizens, besides two hundred and sixty knights. The eight of september, the anniversary of the raising of the siege, is still continued to be celebrated as a general festival throughout the island (*).

Before visiting the different villages of the Island, the attention of the stranger is drawn to the new Cemetery recently constructed near Casal Tarscien, at a little distance from the head of the Grand Harbour. It occupies the whole extent of a hill, and at the top contains a beautiful Church of the Gothic order. This cemetery, which may be considered as one of the finest Necropolis in Europe, was modelled after the Nord cemetery of Paris, and built at a considerable expense. It is destined for the

(*) The chief part of the above sketch has been compiled from vol. II of the " Knights of Malta, " in Constable's Miscollany.

burial of corpses from the four cities, Valletta,
Vittoriosa, Cospicua and Senglea, including
the suburb of Floriana. The place will be greatly embellished by the plantation of trees and
the formation of elegant monuments.

INTERIOR OF THE ISLAND.

Having visited all the interesting places in
the city of Valletta and its suburbs, I shall
proceed to point out what is most deserving of
notice in the remaining part of the island.
But as it is not my intention to describe every
village in the country, which would only be
tedious to the general reader, I shall here-
with subjoin a list of them with their population according to the census taken in the year
1861.

1st District,			Casal Attard	1239
City Notabile and Rabato	5911		— Lia	1371
			— Balzan	662
Casal Dingli	594		4th District,	
2nd District,			Casal Naxaro	2768
Casal Zebbug	4884		— Melleha	975
— Siggieui	2641		— Musta	3828
3rd District,			— Gargur	1200
Casal Birchircara	6202		5th District,	
Sliema	324		Casal Curmi	6197
St. Giuliano	476		— Luca	1592
Misida	1148		— Tarxien	1265

CHURCH OF CASAL MOSTA

Casal Paola	485	Casal Micabiba	894
6th District,		7th District,	
Casal Zurrico	2797	Casal Zeitun	5491
— Crendi	949	— Zabbar	4327
— Safi	286	— Ashiack	1200
— Chircop	409	— Gudia	932

The most remarkable objects of interest in these villages are the parish churches, which are in general well built, commodious,and plentifully ornamented with images and paintings. The Maltese are very liberal in this respect, and seem to vie with one another which shall possess the most splendid house of worship.

Amongst these Parish Churches, the following are remarkable: that of Zeitun, for its beauty and architectural proportions ; that of Zebbug, for its rich decorations and silver treasures ; that of Siggieui, for the elegance of its new portico ; that of Gudia, for its new bell-tower and the measured sound of its bells made in London; and that of Birchircara for its vastness and fine bells. Generally, all the Churches of Malta, except the oldest ones, such as that of Attard, Nasciaro, and the old one of Birchircara, suffer from the decay of architectural taste in the past century: the barocco style every where prevails.

The new Church at Musta deserves the attention of the visitor. It is a round Temple, equal in vastness to the Pantheon at Rome. Its Dome is as wonderful as its beauty and the

harmony of its majestic architecture. It is one
of the most remarkable modern monuments of
Christianity. Its construction was commenced
in 1832 and finished in 1862 on the designs of
the late talented Architect, Mr. Giorgio Gro-
gnet de Vassè, a Maltese who is buried in the
same Church projected by him and raised by
the inhabitants of that village.

All the villages are divided into seven districts
and in every one there is stationed a Syndic,
or sheriff, who has a certain number of police
under his command for the preservation of the
peace. This officer is authorized to act as magistrate, and may decide any civil cause, within
the limits of his jurisdiction, not including a
value of more than £ 5.

An appeal may be made from this court to
that of three Magistrates in Valletta—These
Courts of the Syndics have no criminal jurisdiction.

The common vehicle lately used for travelling
in Malta was called a *calesse;* a kind of carriage
with two wheels, drawn by one horse or mule.
Some of these conveyances are intended for
two persons only, others carry four. The dri-
ver is obliged to walk or run at the side, and
with a small piece of wood, called a *niggiesa,* in
which two short nails are fixed, pricks the animal in order to urge him onward. The roads
in the country, especially those leading to the
principal villages, are in general sufficiently

good for the run of these vehicles; but in the uninhabited parts, they are rugged, and in some cases travelling on horseback would be dangerous. The hire of a good horse for a day is about five shillings, the same price is generally paid for a calesse.

Of late years however carriages have almost entirely replaced the calesses, and in the begining of the year 1857 an Omnibus company was established as a means of conveyance between Valletta and the principal Casals and *vice versa*.

Having made these preliminary observations, I shall imagine the traveller leaving Port des Bombes, and taking the principal road, called St. Giusèppe towards the Old City. After proceeding for about two miles, he will reach a long succession of arches which form part of

THE ACQUEDUCT.

This stupenduous work was begun in the year 1610, during the reign of the Grandmaster Alofio Wignacourt, and was completed in the space of five years. Previous to its erection, in case of scarcity of water in summer, owing to little rain having fell during winter, the inhabitants of the town were obliged to transport water from a spring at the end of the Great Harbour, called *Ain Filep*, which made it very expensive and inconvenient. In order to provide a sufficient supply several springs were united together by subterraneous conduits, and their waters made to flow into one channel. The chief spring rises at a place callad *Diar Chandul*, about two miles west of Città Vecchia. As far as Casal Attard the acqueduct is underground, it afterwards alternately rises and falls with the unevenness of the ground, until it reaches the city. The whole length of its course is about nine and a half English miles.

To this Aqueduct were lately added the waters found in the vicinity of Casal Curmi and discovered near Casal Dingli. The water found at the Marsa, which is somewhat saltish, being too near the sea, is conveyed through iron tubes to the Grand Harbour and Burmola, where it is distributed for the use of the inhabitants. Some steam-pumps draw that water from the cisterns, the supply of which is almost equal to one third of that of the Wignacourt Aqueduct to which new springs were added to increase the supply of water.

———

About five miles from Valletta, a little to the right of the San Giuseppe road, are the

GARDENS AND PALACE OF ST. ANTONIO,

built by the Grandmaster De Paula, and afterwards appropriated as a country-seat by his successors. The palace is spacious and commodious, and the situation exceedingly pleasant. The garden is extensive and contains a great abundance of fruit trees, laid out in a very neat and regular order. The numerous ponds and fountains which are met with in the paved walks, and which may be made to scatter out water in different directions, add considerably to the interest of the place; one may easily have access to these gardens.

The Governor Sir W. Reid has added to these gardens a small agrarian museum, as also an agricultural school for the inhabitants of the country.

LUNATIC ASYLUM.

The new Lunatic Asylum, a work inaugurated by Governor More O'Ferrall, and finished, under the administration of Sir G. Le Marchant is situated at about a mile distant from this Villa, on the road leading to Città Vecchia. This vast building is one of the most beautiful in Europe, for the excellent order of its construction, the perfection of its regulations, and the luxury of its accomodation. The Asylum, which was formerly a simple house at Floriana, is now a large and regular establishment, lying in the declivity of the valley of *Wied Incita*, a lonely, pleasant, and quiet abode of so many unfortunate beings, formerly treated with almost brutal cruelty. It has a plentiful supply of water from the Wignacourt Aqueduct.

r

CITTA' VECCHIA or LA NOTABILE.

Leaving St. Antonio, and passing through Casal Attard, where there is a fine church, half an hour's ride will bring the traveller to the old City, situated on one of the most elevated parts of the island, and nearly in its centre. It is surrounded with walls, and defended with bastions and other modern fortifications, which render it exceedingly strong. Before the arrival of the Arabs, a much more extensive space was enclosed within the walls, but it was diminished by them in order to render its defence more easy and practicable.

In early times this city bore the same name with the island, and was called Melita according to a quotation from Ptolemy the Geographer, lib. iv. c. 3. " Insulæ in alto Mari Pelagiæ hæ sunt, Melite insulæ, in qua civitas Melitæ et Chersonesus et Junonis templum, et Herculis templum. " Upon the Authority of Cicero and Diodorus Siculus we learn that the capital of Malta contained many stately buildings, and was very rich in the style of its architecture. This evidence is substantiated by several remains, which are still seen scattered about the city, and by the vestiges of ancient baths, and temples which have occasionally been found whilst excavating, both within the walls and about the suburbs.

During the domination of the Order of St.

John, this city was governed by a *Hakem* or Ruler, chosen yearly by the Grandmaster, from among the principal Maltese citizens. He was ordinarily called the *Captain of the Rod*, and the jurisdiction of his court extended over the civil and criminal cases of all the villages in the island. The Magistracy of the city consisted of three officers, called *Giurati*, who were also chosen annually by the sovereign. The civil Court was formed of a tribunal of three Judges one of whom judged all regular lawsuits, while the remaining two, called *Idioti*, were only permitted to decide upon certain causes of small moment.

On the election of a new Grandmaster, the ceremony of inauguration was performed in this city. Early in the morning, the sovereign left Valletta, accompanied by his court, and escorted by a body guard with bands of music. On his arrival near the city, he was saluted by the musketry and by the principal *Giurato*, who presented him with a bunch of artificial flowers with an appropriate speech, and afterwards kissed his hand. The procession then proceeded until it joined the Bishop and the clergy, who came out to meet them. The Grandmaster was afterwards placed under a canopy bore on four poles by the *Giurati*, and continued walking until he arrived at the gates of the city, where a place was prepared for him to kneel upon, before which a cross was erected. After the gates were shut, the first *Giurato* stepped forward, bearing in his hand a silver dish, with two keys laid upon it of the same metal, and making a very low bow, addressed the sovereign in the following words. " Most Serene Lord, the Divine Majesty has been pleased to favour us and this city by placing over us so great a prince as lord and master; and the high honor is conferred upon me of presenting to Your Serene Highness the keys of this city, in order that you may take possession thereof. Therefore, my colleagues and myself, in all humility, beg of Your Most Serene Highness to deign to swear upon the habit of the Grand Cross, that you will observe all the privileges, and franchises, and usages of this city, and of the Island of Malta, which were conceded to them by the Most Serene Sovereigns of Arragon and Sicily, and by the magnanimous Grandmasters of this sacred Order, the predecessors of Your Most Serene Highness, and command that the same be observed. " The Grandmaster then laid his hand upon the cross on his breast, and said : "I am bound to do so ; I swear. " After the keys were delivered into his hand, the procession proceeded to the Cathedral, where a solemn *Te Deum* was sung, and after the celebration of Mass, the pageant terminated.

The ceremony of consecrating the bishops is also performed in the Cathedral of this city.

The Cathedral and the ancient Magisterial Palace are the chief objects worthy of notice within the walls of the city. The site of the former building, according to tradition, was formerly occupied by the residence of Publius, who was governor of the Island, at the time of St. Paul's shipwreck. The edifice is built in Corinthian style, and contains an altar composed of several kinds of very rich marble. In the upper part of the building there is a small library, and a few antiquities which have been found from time to time in excavations made about the city. The extensive view of the Island from the terrace of the Cathedral is exceedingly fine, as it almost takes in the whole country. This Church was greatly damaged by the severe shock of earthquake experienced in Malta on the 12th October 1856. The ancient Magisterial Palace is a commodious building, now turned into a Hospital for military invalids, under the name of *Sanatorium*.

Besides the cathedral there are two convents in the city, one a monastery of Benedictine nuns, annexed to which is a small but neat church.

The bishop's Palace and Theological Seminary are situated close by the cathedral, and are worthy of notice. In the Saloon there is a gallary of Portraits of the Bishops of this dioceso. Adjoining the latter building is the supposed site of the ancient temple of Apollo.

The suburbs of the city, called *Rabbato*, contain several large buildings, among which are four monasteries, and two hospitals, one called *Della Saura* administered by the Bishop and the other dedicated to *Santo Spirito*. The former was founded by several legacies left by pious individuals, and the latter appears to have been a public establishment instituted at a very early period. It is at present under the direction of the local government.

ST. PAUL'S CAVE.

One of the most interesting objects in the suburbs of Città Vecchia is the Grotto of St. Paul, situate underneath a Church dedicated to the same saint. According to tradition, St. Paul, accompanied by Luke the Apostle, and Trophimus, resided in this cave for the space of three months, the time of his stay upon the island. In order to give the tradition some appearance of consistency a famous writer on Malta assigns Paul's "modesty and humility" as the reason of his choosing such a habitation; for it cannot be supposed, argues the same writer that the barbarous inhabitants, who manifested their kindness in so signal a manner to the apostle, or that the most noble and courteous Publius, who was so greatly indebted to him, would have willingly suffered Paul to occupy so mean a dwelling. Nor can it be imagined that the apostle was here kept prisoner, after the centurion had forbid the soldiers to kill any of the criminals, whom he had brought with him, in order to save Paul's life.

The veneration of this cave very much increased about the begining of the seventeenth century, when a citizen of Cordova, named Fra Giovanni, left his native country, and came to Malta in order to tenant it. This anachorite had a chapel erected over the grotto of St. Paul, dedicated to St. Publius, which was afterwards very much enlarged by the Grandmaster Lascaris and enriched with donations of a vast number of relics by the reigning Pontiffs of Rome. Among these Ciantar enumerates a piece of the true cross on which Christ was crucified, some remains of six of the apostles, and of about fifty other saints.

The descent to the grotto is by a convenient staircase, leading down from the chapel. The grotto itself is of a concave and circular form, not more than twelve yards in diameter, and about eight feet high in the centre. A fine marble statue of St. Paul, with a latin inscription, occupies the middle of the cave, before which several lights are kept continually burning. The material of which the grotto is formed is a soft magnesian lime-stone and reckoned very efficacious as a febrifuge.

On the right of the entrance is the following inscription, placed there by the Grandmaster Emmanuel Pinto.

D. O. M.

Hoc dextrum divi Pauli cryptae latus,
terram asportantibus numquam clausum,
et numquam deficiens, semper excisum et
numquam decrescens, ut in majorem
cresceret venerationem, eminentissimus
H. O. M. M. et Princeps seren. Fr. D.
Emman. Pinto nobiliori auxit ornatu
MDCCXLVIII.

The opinion is quite common among the natives, that the stone of which this cave is composed is continually regenerating, and that although a sufficient quantity has been taken away
to load several vessels, the dimensions of the cave
remain precisely the same. It would be useless
to adduce here any proofs to shew the glaring
absurdity and inconsistency of this opinion;
such tales passed current during the ignorance
of the dark ages, but the common sense of the
present day will treat them as fables. A miraculous agency is assigned for the above phenomenon, as this at once removes every objection
which may be brought against it from any natural cause.

A small Church, dedicated to St. Publius, is
built, on this grotto, and divine service is performed in it by the collegians resident in a
contiguous convent supported out of a fund
bequeathed by the Order and now administered
by the Government. The priests of this Collegiate Church are at present the only clergy-

men in the island who wear the octagon cross
of the Knights of Malta, besides the nuns of
St. Ursola of Valletta.

On the other side of St. Paul's Church there
is a square, in the middle of which stands a
statue of the Apostle, who according to tradition, preached to the inhabitants of these Islands from that place. Underneath there are
many graves, wherein lie the remains of illustrious foreigners, who wished to be buried within
these precincts.

CATACOMBS.

The Catacombs of St. Paul are situated about
five minutes walk from the Church, whither
the sacristan generally accompanies all travellers with a supply of tapers, which he lights
before entering. The descent to the entrance
is about nine feet deep, by staircase three feet
wide, leading to a kind sf gallery dug under
ground, with a great number of others branch-
ing off from the principal, and also from the
secondaries. The sides of these passages contain many niches to receive the body, cut in the
walls without any regular order: some are entirely uncovered; while others are arranged with
more order, in two stories, and partly closed
with a layer of mortar raised up in a circular
form. These sepulchres are of different sizes,
some proportionably formed for infants, which
generally occupy the sides, whilst in many of

the larger ones, it may be seen from a couple of circular holes sufficiently large to receive the head, that they were intended for two full-grown persons.

There are several halls among these galleries; the roof of one is supported by a group of rough fluted columns, and on the floor of the same are two circular blocks, about four feet in diameter, flat on the top, with a low edge round the circumference. Some are of opinion that the latter were used for washing the bodies before burial.

The area of these subterraneous excavations cannot now be determined, as many of the passages have been walled up, lest the curious visitant should lose himself in such a labyrinth, which according to tradition has several times happened. The stone of which these catacombs are formed is very soft and porous, and consumes away very fast by the dampness which prevails so low underground.

Besides the above there are other similar excavations in the Città Notabile, many of which have been closed up. One of them, however, called by the natives *Abbatia*, in the district of *Bir Riebu*, about a quarter of a mile outside the suburbs, still remains open. The descent to the principal part of these catacombs is from a well at a few paces distant from one of the subterraneous apartments. About fifteen feet below the surface of the earth is a regular door way,

in which there has been a wooden door. After
passing the threshold, there is a chamber about
19 feet long by 14 wide, excavated in the rock
which is rather soft, the roof being supported
by an arch and two pillars formed in excavating.
The chamber contains several sepulchres, and a
round block similar to that which I have mentioned in the catacombs of St. Paul.

Upon the arch over the farthest sepulchre,
there is an inscription, of which the following
is all that can be deciphered.

```
        N O T
        N                    i T O
B I ⋈ I T I N P A C
    P A C E M A N I S T      A C V
        A T I O              PoSITAE
    INHoCAOCO                RECOR
```

From the tenor of what can be gathered
from the above, it may be concluded, that it
was the work of Christians.

There is generally much extravagance in the
opinions entertained concerning the original
design of these, as well as other subterraneous
sepulchral excavations. Many will have that
they were formed by the primitive christians,
who, during times of persecution, lived and
buried the bodies of their confessors and martyrs in them. This opinion prevails at Rome,
and consequently a number of labourers are
kept constantly at work at the catacombs, and
as soon as they discover a repository with any

of the marks of its being that of a saint, what is found within is immediately taken care of. The principal mark of its sanctity is a small projection in the side of the gallery, a little below the repository, which sometimes contains pieces of phials, tinctured with various colours, in which it is pretended that the blood of the martyrs was preserved, in order to distinguish them from others. This imposition has no foundation to support it, and I would just remark, that the same custom prevails unto the present day in some places of Asia Minor. While at Castro Rosso on the coast of Caramania, I observed several small mud-hillocks, piled up above the graves, in which were fixed small pieces of broken glass and earthenware of various colours.

Against the above opinion, concerning the design of these catacombs, it may be justly argued, that at a time when Christians were openly persecuted, it was not at all probable, that such vast undertakings could have been carried on without the knowledge of the persecutors, nor that any inimical government would have permitted the work to be prosecuted in opposition to their own proceedings. If, again these were completed during season of peace, they must have been public, and being found in such exposed situations, just without the city, would never have been useful for a place of refuge.

It is my opinion, that the catacombs of Malta were originally the work of the Phœnicians, or the Romans, whose general manner it was to bury in caves ; nor was the custom of interring as we do now, in the open air, or in churches, ever made use of before christianity introduced it. The Romans probable derived the custom of burying their dead in such subterraneous cemeteries from the Phœnicians; for, that the same was prevalent with them, is very evident from the numerous catacombs to be found in Rome. At length, however, they derived from the Greeks the manner of burning their dead bodies, and as this came gradually into general use, the catacombs fell into total neglect. In this state, we may suppose that the Christians took possession of them in times of persecution, where they concealed themselves because it was not so likely that they would be searched after in such abandoned places. When the empire became christian, they again fell into that state of disuse in which they are found at present. (*)

ANCIENT TOMBS OF BINGEMMA.

About one hour's walk to the west of Città Vecchia is a hill called *ta Bingemma,* in which are cut a number of sepulchral grots, of different sizes, and varying in their internal forma-

(*) See the interesting work on Catacombs and St. Paul' Grotto, by the learned Rev. Giovanni Gatt Said.

tion. At present, many of them are choked up with rubbish, and others serve as sheep-cotes and stables for cattle. Some appear to have been originally intended for one person only, whilst others were designed for two or three as may be seen from the circular inlets made to receive the heads. A little above the tombs are cut small niches in the wall, apparently destined as stands for lamps. The caves occupy one side of the mountain, and are placed one above another to three tiers or rows. Several large caves contain no tombs whatever, and were probably designed for a different purpose.

Some have supposed that this place formed the cemetery of the Essenes, a sect among the Jews, whose principal residence was the west side of the Lake Asphaltites, and whose manner of life was very retired and recluse. Leaving aside the want of all historical evidence to establish the fact, that any number of this sect ever existed on the island, the Arabic name, which the hill has retained, goes somewhat to nullify this supposition. Besides there is another place not far from Città Vecchia, close by the hill called *Emtarfa*, which has preserved, until the present day, the name of Kboor-el-Yehood, the *Graves of the Jews*: hence it is not likely that this people possessed two burial-places so close to each other, or that they ever existed here in such numbers as to render this necessary.

As to the style of the above tombs, very

little can be argued therefrom, since different nations of antiquity buried their dead in the same manner. The small village of Siloah, in the valley of Jehosaphat, consists of huts formed from a number of Jewish sepulchres, cut in the rock at the foot of Mount Olivet, and which bear much resemblance to those of Bingemma. The Sepulchres of the Kings and of the Judges, about a mile to the north of Jerusalem, differ very little in their construction from the catacombs of St. Paul in Città Vecchia. In Persia and Egypt the same custom prevailed, as may be seen from many excavations of the same kind which exist unto the present day.

I have already stated my opinion, in a former part of this work, that these grots are vestiges of the Phœnicians, who held possession of the island for eight centuries. This manner of enterring the dead was quite common to this people, as may be seen from the extensive cemeteries outside the city of Sidon, one of their ancient principal towns. The formation of the interior apartments of the tombs exactly correspond in both places, and the site chosen for the purpose, in the side of a mountain, and not far distant from the city, is equally analogous.

Another coincidence between the tombs of the Phœnicians in Syria, and those of Bingemma, ought not to be overlooked,—a coincidence which does not exist between the latter and Jewish burial-places in the Holy Land : I allude to the larger caves which are found among the tombs, apparently destined for some other purpose than that of interment. I imagine that these were temples, as at a very early period the custom prevailed for men to repair to the summit of hills or else in caverns in rocks, in order to worship the gods, whom they imagined held their residence in such places. This mode of worship existed among the Greeks, as may be known from the cavern which was dedicated to Aphrodite in Phocis, and the situation of Delphi and Parnassus, of which latter Strabo writes : (lib. ix. p. 638) " The mountain of Parnassus is a place of great reverence, having *many caverns,* and other detached spots highly honoured and sanctified." Among the Persians most of their temples were caverns in rocks, either formed by nature, or artificially produced. Porphyry assures us, that the Deity had always a rock or cavern for his temple ; and that these existed amongst tombs may be argued from the testimony of Thevenot (Part 2nd p. 144, 146) who found several stone coffins among the excavated temples of the Persians. From these data it may be argued that the same custom amongst the Phœnicians, and that the similarity of the tombs of Bingemma, in every respect corresponding with those which undoubtedly belonged to this ancient people, establishes them as the remains of their work in the island of Malta.

The ruins of the ancient temples are worthy of a visit. On the eastern side of the Island, near the bay of Bir-zebbugia, there exist the vestiges of the famous temple of Hercules: they consist of large irregular and polygon stones piled up one upon the others opposite these ruins, near the sea side, there is a vestibule composed of only three stones, the largest of which is about 16 feet long.

About a mile distant to the south of Crendi, are the ruins of another Phœnician temple, dedicated to the Brothers Kabiri constructed of cyclopic stones. In the course of the excavations made in 1839, statues, bones, and an altar were found, and are now preserved in the museum of the Public Library.

About another mile distant from these ruins there are the remains of another large temple, dedicated to the worship of Esculapius. It is called *Mnaidra*, that is, a temple of light, and the other one just mentioned is styled *Hagiar Kim*. Other marks of cyclopic constructions exist in various parts of the Island, amongst which those on Corradino Hill and a large cistern on the road *tal Medewiet*, at a little distance from the temple of Hercules are remarkable.

The village Zurrico contains the remains of a Grecian construction and a sepulchre, which are very well preserved in the residence of the Parish-priest. Similar vestiges are also to be found on the road leading from this village to the neighbouring one of Safi.

EMTAHLEB.

This place is situated not far distant from the shore, about three miles to the west of Città Vecchia, and is much resorted to in the summer season by parties of pleasure. The little variety of hill and dale which this spot presents, and the comparative fertility of the vallies, watered by a copious spring, together with a delightful prospect of the sea, form the attractions which draw visitors occasionally to spend a day here. There are only a few houses at this place, but a tolerable spacious cave through which a spring of limpid water runs, serves as a very agreable retreat from the heat of the sun, and as a commodious dining room in which to spread out a rural repast.

BOSCHETTO.

The above name is given to a public garden, situated in a delightful valley, about two miles to the south of Città Vecchia. This place is well worth visiting. The garden is watered by numerous canals, which are supplied from the principal acqueduct. Here is likewise a commodious artificial grotto, with a fine fountain at the end, and provided with a stone table and benches, forming a pleasant and cool resting-place for a pick-nick party during the heat of summer.

On a hill which overlooks the garden, called Monte Verdala, is a large square edifice, built by the Grandmaster of the same name, in the year 1586. This building was used as a country-seat by his successors, until the Palace and Gardens of St. Antonio were substituted for that purpose by the Grandmaster De Paula.

It is at present in good repair, owing to the work done by order of Governor Sir W. Reid, who had a special liking to this place, he having chosen the Boschetto Palace as a summer residence. Some years back the cultivation of silk worms was introduced in these Islands, and this palace was appropriated for this purpose, but notwithstanding all the efforts used, the plan failed; this accounts for the extensive plantation of mulberry trees in Boschetto and other parts of the island.

On the feast of St. Peter and St. Paul, (29th June) the religious ceremonies of which are celebrated at the Old City, the Gardens of Boschetto present a very joyous appearance. Numerous companies of people from the towns and the surrounding villages meet here, and pass the day in various kinds of rural passtimes and amusements.

Since 1853, through the efforts of Sir William Reid the promoter of agricultural industry, yearly agrarian exhibitions, similar to those held in other parts of Europe, take place in these gardens on the above festival, that being the principal day of meeting for all country people. A similar exhibition takes place in Gozo on the principal festival of that island the Assumption of the Blessed Virgin Mary, the 15th August—These exhibitions are under the direction of a society entitled *La Società Economico Agraria;*—and have had a yearly increasing success.

THE INQUISITOR'S PALACE.

Stands a little to the south of the Boschetto, in a very delightful situation commanding a view of one of the richest vales in Malta. This building was formerly the country-seat of the Inquisitor, but is now the property of the British Government. It is occasionally occupied by some of the gentry of the town, but when tenantless, travellers and persons visiting the place for recreation or pleasure are permitted to use it. The edifice is neat and commodious, and had formerly a small chapel connected with it, which is at present used as a common room.

In the valley below is a large spring, called *Ain il Kbira*, by which name the region around the Palace is known. The fruit produced in this place is very fine. A little to the east is the district called *Giryhenti*, which is likewise very fertile in fruit and other productions. This is also watered by several springs, one of which issues from beneath an ancient building called *Ta Durrensi*. A little below the ruin, the water runs through a spacious cave, the area of which has lately been filled up by the falling of the roof. There are several other old buildings in the neighbourhood, one called by the natives *Torre tal Fulia*. Besides these vestiges of antiquity, several hewn stones of uncommon size are to be seen in an old wall above the group of caves situated in the eastern avenue leading to the Inquisitor's Palace, and supposed to have been formerly the residence of a company of gypsies.

FAUARA.

This name is given to a spot on the southern coast which overlook the sea, and was much frequented by the inhabitants as a place of recreation and pleasure. The direct road to it lies through Casal Zebbug and Casal Siggiewi; but by crawling down a steep rock, it can be reached from the Inquisitor's Palace, from which it is about two miles distant. The soil hereabouts is remarkably fertile, and is symmetrically piled up in terraces on the side of the ascent, which rises gradually from a precipice overlooking the sea about two hundred feet high.

Beneath the small church of this place is a

spring which runs through an artificial cave,
and thence flows into a large pond, from whence
it is let out in different directions to water the
land.   This spring is now joined with the Bouverie Aqueduct, which receives the water from
the springs of St. Giorgio and Annunziata, besides the one just mentioned. It runs to an
extent of about seven miles and distributes its
waters to the towns on the other side of the
Grand Harbour, after supplying the tanks of
several villages through which it runs.   In this
cave is a stone table and benches for the accommodation of visitors, who come here to
spend a day of recreation.

From Fauara the traveller may have a good
view of the small island of Filfla, about five
miles distant from the coast. This island is
only inhabited by rabbits, of which there are a
great number. It is occasionally visited by
fishing-boats, which go thither in order to gather the patella, and other shell-fish, which
abound on the shores of the rock.

THE MAKLUBA.

The road to this place lies through Casal Lu-
ca Micabiba, and Crendi, from which last it is
about ten minutes' walk, and in all about seven
miles from Valletta. The name is given to an
oval hollow in the earth, sunk to the distance
of 130 feet, at the bottom of which is a very
pleasant garden consisting of various kinds of

fruit trees. The length of the aperture is 330 feet, and the width 200. The descent to the area below is by a narrow and very rugged staircase, cut into the circumference. The appearance of the inner sides is very craggy; the rocks around are broken and scattered in every direction, and the whole face of the land around this quarter bears evident signs that it once underwent some violent concussion. The country in the vicinity begins to decline irregularly for the distance of two or three miles before it centres in this spot, which very abruptly sinks into a deep hollow. It is difficult to determine what may have been the natural causes productive of these phenomena; but the most probable opinion is, that they are occasioned by the destruction of a subterraneous cave in the event of an earthquake, or some other violent convulsion of nature. The word *Makluba* signifies *overturned*, and the common tradition is, that this hollow was the site of an ancient village, the inhabitants of which, like those of Sodom and Gomorrah, vexed the Almighty until he took vengeance upon them by destroying their village, as He did the tents of Dathan and Abiram, by causing the earth to open and swallow it up. According to Ciantar, some bitumen was formerly found here in the remains of a cistern, none of which, however, appears at present. During winter, the water in the cavity sometimes covers the trees, but it soon

finds an outlet through the fissures of the rock.
Close by the cave is a small chapel dedicated to
St. Matthew.

The appearance of the rocks above the sea
coast, a little beyond Makluba, confirms the
idea that it was produced by some violent natural commotion. The stone is of a dark hue,
and is very rough and craggy. There are also
large ravines formed in the rock, which open
in the direction of the sea, and run very narrow
towards the bottom.

GHAR HASSAN.

This Cave is situated on the southern coast
of the Island, and is well worth visiting, on
account of its interesting locality, and the peculiar style of its formation. The chief entrance
stands upon a perpendicular rock, about two
hundred feet above the level of the sea, the
descent to which is rather dangerous. The interior is divided into several natural recesses,
stretching out in various directions, and extending inwards for a considerable distance. A
narrow passage across the cave leads round to
another opening overlooking the sea, which
cannot be reached in any other manner. There
still exists a tradition among the natives, that
this place took its name from a Saracen who
resided in it for some time after the expulsion
of his countrymen from Malta. It is rather a
singular coincidence, that the same name is

mentioned in the Cufic inscription found in the island some time back, of which Ciantar gives a copy in his *Malta Illustrata* plate xvii. A very ingenious translation of the above, by the Cavalier d' Itlalinsky, Minister Extraordinary and Plenipotentiary of the Emperor of Russia, may be seen in the *Mines de l' Orient*, tom. i. p. 395.

An illustrious Italian writer, an exile in Malta, wrote an excellent Canto in 1846, which well deserves a perusal.

HERMITAGE OF ST. PAUL.

About a mile to the left of the road, after leaving Casal Nasshar, there is an extensive ravine called by the natives *Uied-el-Asel*, in the sides of which are several natural caves of tolerable dimensions. On a ledge of the rock, rather high up in the ravine, is a small chapel dedicated to St. Paul, built upon the spot where he is said to have resided. Were it not for the natural grandeur of the scene around; this tradition could communicate but little interest to the locality in question; as a proof of which I shall relate the following anecdote. It is now about two months since I visited the hermitage in company with a friend of mine, and while resting on the little square before the chapel, I asked a countryman, who has brought us a few grapes to purchase, wether he thought St. Paul ever lived there. He very quaintly replied:

Q

" Sir, I do not know; there are so many places
on the island where people say that the apostle
resided, that I am inclined to think, that these
spots, were only honoured by a visit from him.
And then again, to imagine, that some followed him to mark these spots, during his short
residence in Malta, is rather too much for me
to believe." This I regard as a specimen of native common sense.

Within the chapel of the Hermitage there is
a cistern, filled with the water which trickles
down from the adjacent rock. Several of the
Grandmasters of the Order were accustomed
to have their tables supplied from this spring.

After crossing over the extensive and fertile
plain of Nasshar, the next place of interest in
this direction is

ST. PAUL'S BAY.

According to a tradition of the natives, this
is the place where the great Apostle of the
Gentiles was shipwrecked, while on his voyage
from Syria to Rome. The bay is about three
miles in length, and two in width at the entrance,
gradually decreasing towards the extremity.
At this point the beach is sandy, and differs
from the general appearance of the coast round
the harbour, which is rugged and rocky. To
the north-west of the entrance is a small oblong
island, called *Selmone* or *Selmoon*, separated
from the mainland by a narrow straight. A

tower and other fortifications in the vicinity serve to defend the bay, and were raised for that purpose by the Knights of Malta.

The only object of interest worth noticing in this place is a small chapel, built upon the supposed site where the barbarians lighted a fire to warm the shipwrecked crew. It contains several old drawings, illustrative of the events connected with the landing of St. Paul in this quarter.

As it has been disputed by several writers whether Malta, or Meleda in the Adriatic sea, was the island where St. Paul was cast away, both which were then called Melita, I do not judge it out of place, to bring forward under this head the arguments which have been adduced in favour of Meleda, and at the same time to subjoin my own reasons for maintaining the contrary. The scriptural narrative of the event in Acts of the Apostles c. xxvii, the reader may refer to.

The following question is extracted chiefly from a *Disertation of the voyage of St. Paul,* written by Dr. Falconer of Bath, containing the most plausible objections to the common received opinion on the subject, which I have ever met with.

"That this island was *Meleda,* near the Illyrian coast, not *Malta,* on the southern coast of Sicily, may appear from the following consideration.

" 1. It lies confessedly in the *Adriatic* sea, but *Malta* a considerable distance from it.

" 2. It lies nearer the mouth of the *Adriatic* than any other island of that sea; and would, of course, be more likely to receive the wreck of any vessel driven by tempests towards that quarter. And it lies N. W. by N. of the south-west promontory of Crete; and came nearly in the direction of a storm from the south-east quarter.

" 3. An obscure island called *Melita*, whose inhabitants were " barbarous," was not applicable to the celebrity of *Malta* at that time, which *Cicero* represents as abounding in curiosities and riches, and possessing a remarkable manufacture of the finest linen.   Orat. in Verrem, iv. § 18. 56.   See more fully on this subject, the citation from *Diodorus Siculus* on p. 4.

" 4. The circumstance of the viper, or venomous snake, which fastened on St. Paul's hand, agrees with the damp and woody island of *Meleda*, affording shelter and proper nourishment for such; but not with the dry and rocky island of *Malta* in which there are no serpents now and none in the time of Pliny.

" 5. The disease with which the father of *Publius* was affected, (verse 8) *Dysentery* combined with *fever*, (probably intermittent) might well suit a country woody and damp, and probably, from want of draining, exposed to the putrid effluvia of confined moisture; but was not likely to affect a dry, rocky, and remarkably healthy island like *Malta*.

Ver. 12. "After a stay of three months, they departed, probably about the begining of March, in a ship of Alexandria, which had wintered also in the isle, and perhaps from similar stress of weather, and came from thence to *Syracuse*, where they spent three days, and thence proceeded to *Rhegium*, on the straits of *Messina*, and after a day's stay they reached *Puteoli* in two days, which was the usual port at which the corn ships from Egypt landed their cargoes. Here, also *Josephus* and his shipwrecked companions landed, after they were taken up by a *Cyrenian* vessel, the year after St. Paul's voyage." (See Hale's Analysis, Vol. I. p. 468, 469.)

The argument contained in the first objection is based chiefly upon the word *Adria*, mentioned in the 27th verse; but Bochart, Beza, Grothius and others, have shewn, that at the time in question, was comprehended under that name the whole of the sea between Greece, Italy and Africa; so that it comprised the Ionian, Cretan, and Sicilian seas. See Hesychius, " *Ionium mare quod nunc Adria.*" And Again Procop. lib. I. *Insulae Gaulus* (Gozo) *et Melitu Adriaticum et Tuscum pelagum disterminant.*

The first clause of the second objection is entirely hypothetical, and would only serve to increase the testimony in favour of *Meleda* in

the Adriatic, after it has been once proved to
be the landing-place of St. Paul by superior argument. The second clause, however, takes
too much for granted. It assumes that the
Euroclydon is the south-east wind, and then
draws an inference accordingly. This word,
which occurs only in the passage before us,
has exercised the learning and acumen of many
generations of cities. Numerous conjectures have
raised concerning it, and several changes proposed; but before conjecture be resorted to, we
ought to see what account can be given of the
common term. The nearest approach to it is
Euroclydon, given in a citation of Baissom
from *Const. Manass. Chron.* 104, which seems
to mean *violently tempestuous*. Several other
writers have shewn that the Euroclydon was
not a *point wind*, but rather a kind of hurricane
or whirlwind, often shifting its quarter, and
tossing them backwards and forwards. This
exactly agrees with what the Italian sailors
call a *tuffone*, and the English a *Levanter*, which
blows from the N. E. and E. and is the most
tempestuous wind in the Mediterranean, especially during the autumnal equinox, the time
when Paul was at sea.

The above receives additional weight from
the 13th verse, where it is said, "But not long
after there arose against *it.*" it is difficult to
determine to what noun the particle *it* should
here be referred : the nearest is the word 'Crete'

in the preceeding verse; but this would be
harsh and unnatural. My idea is, that the
word *ship* is understood ; and if so, Euroclydon
could not have been the south east wind for that
instead of being 'against them,' would have
been in their favour.

The narrative proceeds : " And when the
ship was caught, and could not bear up into
the wind, we let her drive. " &c. And v. 27.
" When the *fourteenth night* was come, as we
were driven up and down in Adria, about *midnight* the shipmen deemed that they drew near
to some country." It appears from this account
that during fourteen days they were driven by
a tempestuous wind, without discovering any
land. If, however, they had been driven in a
direction to arrive at Meleda, they would have
passed close by the Morea, the Ionian islands,
and through the strait between Italy and
Greece ; and this, not in a direct line, but with
some windings ; and it is higly improbable, not
say impossible, that they should not have discovered any where the vicinity of land, as well
as they discovered the vicinity of the island
where they landed, even " about midnight. "
Further, " although neither sun nor stars in
many days appeared," yet they certainly could
find out the quarter in which the sun rose and
set, and from it could discover in which direction the wind drove them. Finding that it was
blowing from the south-east, they would of

course have looked for some anchorage in Greece, and the Ionian islands, where they would have arrived in a few days. Besides, we know that the south-east wind, in the Mediterranean never continues so long in winter, and is seldom so tempestuous as the east wind, supposing then that it was the east wind, it would in fourteen days have carried them in a strait direction to Malta, without seeing and even without expecting to see any land.

The third argument adduced by the objector is not valid, inasmuch as it is a well known fact that the pride of the Greeks, and afterwards of the Romans, accounted men of all other nations barbarians. The apostle Paul makes use of the same expressions in I Cor. xiv. 11 : If I know not the meaning of the voice, I shall be unto him that speaketh a *barbarian,* and he that speaketh shall be a *barbarian,* unto me." Herdotus also, lib. II. 158 says: The Egyptians call all those *barbarians,* who have not the same language with themselves. " And again Ovid, " *Barbarus* hic ego sum, quia not intelligor ulli. " *In trist.* ver. 10. These remarks, however, will not apply to Meleda, which was situated in a well known part and most probably inhabited by people who spoke the Greek language.

The fourth argument respects the viper which fastened on St. Paul's hand, the existence of which the objector judges to agree more with the damp and woody island of Meleda, than with the dry soil of Malta. All this I am ready to allow, as also the testimony of Pliny, that there were no *venemous* serpents on this island in his time; but that there never were nor are *any* serpents in Malta is false. I myself have often seen snakes six feet long and I know positively, that the same animals, of a smaller dimension, are very common in the country. They are very harmless, but show some tokens of rage when irritated. It is my opinion, that one of these creatures is meant in the text, and that the very uncommon manner in which it laid hold at the hand of the apostle, (a fact the inhabitants had never before witnessed) was the cause of their evil surmisings, and of their anticipations of the consequence. How far there may have been a divine interposition in causing the animal to act as it did, I cannot say; very likely it was only the novel effect of the fire.

The fifth objection contains but little plausibility; for, it is not necessary that a disease should be endemic in order to the existence of *one* case, which, however, we are almost obliged to infer from the argument of the objector. But, moreover, it is a well known fact, and the very disease with which Publius was afflicted is by no means uncommon in this island during autumn.

The last paragraph is not brought forward as an argument, and it is well that it is not. The

narrative of St. Luke says, that they first went
to Syracuse, then to Rhegium, now Reggio on
the southern point of Calabria, and next to
Puteoli near the present Naples. This is the
natural course in going from Malta to Rome;
but coming from the Adriatic sea it is not at
all probable, that they should first have gone
down to Syracuse, and then have turned back
again to Reggio.

Another incidental proof against the opinion
I am endeavouring to confute is the fact, that
at the island where the apostle was shipwrecked,
there was another vessel, which had put in on
her way to Rome, in order there to winter.
Now it is certain more probable, that the Melita here spoken of is our Malta, and not the
Meleda in the Archipelago, the former being
quite in the way, while the latter lies several
miles out of the regular course to that city.

The description given of the shore by the
sacred historian gives little satisfaction to the
enquirer; yet it proves nothing against its
being Malta. " And when it was day, they
knew not the land but they discovered a certain creek with a shore, " is all that St. Luke
writes.

But the 41st verse is not so easy to be understood: the word in the original, (διθαλασσος)
rendered 'two seas,' is as sometimes applied to
an isthmus which divides two seas, just as the
Latin *bimaris*; sometimes to long peninsulas

jutting out into the sea, and also to spits of sand under water. The latter seems to be the most probable idea, for we are told that the forepart of the vessel struck fast and remained immoveable, but the hinder part was broken with the violence of the waves. This took place in consequence of their intention to thrust in the ship, when they unfortunately lighted upon a sand bank, where the sea is generally rough and surfy. Some cities understand the passage as conveying the idea of a surf or eddy, which beat upon the stere of the vessel, while the head remained fast aground. And others again have imagined, that the *two seas* refer to the channels, which run on each side the small island of Salamone, and which meet in the harbour of St. Paul.

To the above proofs in favour of Malta being the island where the Great Apostle was cast away, we may mention the tradition which has existed amongst the natives from time immemorial; an item of considerable weight when combined with other concurrent testimony.

St. Paul's Bay is now a watering place, where many of the inhabitants pass the summer months.

MELLEHA and CALYPSO'S GROTTO.

About an hour's ride from St. Paul's bay brings the traveller to the Church of Melleha, a place very much frequented by the devout among the Maltese, and by no means displeasing as to its situation. It is partly cut out of the solid rock, and contains a great number of presents to the Vrigin, to whom the building is dedicated, such as silver and waxen limbs, pieces of old cable, iron chains and fetters, pictures representing the deliverance of the distressed, &c. Over the small altar is a drawing of St. Mary, underneath which it is pretended that there is an original portrait of the same executed by St. Luke the *Physician.* Several authors take it for granted, that this apostle, who accompanied Paul in some of his travels, came with him also to Malta : the grounds of such an opinion I have never had the good fortune to see established by historical evidence.

Round a spacious square in front of the church is a row of rooms, prepared for the reception of devout visitors, snd occasionally serve also for the accomodation of the parties of pleasure which often resort to this place. Just below the church is a small cave, called the *Grotta della Madonna,*in which there is a spring of water, surmounted by a large stone statue of the Virgin. It is firmly believed by many of the people, that this image has been several times taken up and offered a more respectable place of the church, but that during the night, she has again chosen to return down forty stairs to her own old position. In this cave there are a few other headless statues, which may possibly have been heathen gods and goddesses. According to the testimony of the sacristan, they owe their decapitation to the infidel rage of the French, during their short occupation of the island.

On the opposite side of the dale, which lies between the Church of Melleha and a range of hig hrugged rocks, are many caves, some formed naturally, and other cut by art. On examining a few of these, I found evident signs that they had once been inhabited : the floors of several are well smoothed, small niches for lamps are seen in the walls, and apparent divisions in the larger excavations for the constructions of chambers. A little previous to my last visit to this spot, a countryman discovered a small lachrymatory and lamp, while digging in one of these grottos. Both are made of red clay, resembling those in the Public Library, and apparently of Phœnician origin, if I may judge from their shape. The lachrymatory is in the possession of the priest of Melleha, the lamp I obtained myself from the countryman.

Melleha, recently made a Parish, has now become a popolous village, having hotels and restaurants with the requisite accommodations for visitors.

About half a mile to the west of the church of Melleha is the supposed Grotto of Calypso, the spot so enchantingly sung by Homer, and

R

dilated upon by Fenelon in his 'Aventures de
Telemaque.' It is situated at the foot of a hill
in which are many other grots of different dimensions, the greater part of which are still
occupied by the peasants of the neighbourhood.
A spring of clear water runs through the cave
of the goddess, and from thence flows forth into a large basin, from which it is let out to
fertilize the delightful garden just below. Of
this spot Homer writes in his Fifth Book:

Large was the grot in which the nymph he found,
(The fair hair'd nymph with every beauty crown'd)
She sat and sung; the rocks resound her lays;
The cave was brighten'd with a rising blaze:
Cedar and frankincense, an odorous pile,
Flam'd on the hearth, and wide perfum'd the isle;
While she with work and song the time divides,
And through the loom the golden shuttle guides.
Without the grot, a various silvan scene
Appear'd around, and groves of living green:
Poplars and alders ever quivering play'd,
And nodding cypress form'd a fragrant shade;
On whose high branches, waving with the storm,
The birds of broadest wing their mansion form.
The cough, the sea-mew, the loquacious crow,
And scream aloft, and skim the deeps below.
Depending vines the shelving cavern screen,
With purple clusters blushing through the green.
Four limpid fountains from the clefts distil,
And every fountain pours a sev'ral rill,

In mazy winding wandering down the hill:
Where bloomy meads with vivid greens were crowned
And glowing violets threw odours round.
A scene, where, if a god should cast his sight,
A god might gaze, and wonder with delight!

Embellished and decorated by the masterly
pen of the poet, a miserable cave is converted
into a fit residence for a fabulous goddess.
However, any admirer of natural scenery will
be delighted with the prospect which stretches
before the sight from the summit of this hill.
The green spot beneath, washed at its base
by the Bay of Melleha, the islands of Gozo
and Comino in the distance, and the rugged
heights around, form a *coup d' oeil* not every
where to be enjoyed in the island of Malta.

About one hour's ride, over a rather rough
road, brings you to the place called

MARFA.

This is the termination of the island on the
norh-west, and from this spot it is usual for
those to embark, who wish to visit Gozo, and
who prefer a shorter sea voyage than going
in a boat direct from Malta. At Marfa there
is a small country house, which has been occasionally occupied by the Governors of the
island.

Midway in the channel which separates Malta from Gozo, called the *Straits of Fregi*, is the small

ISLAND OF COMINO

formerly called *Hephaestia* or *Phaestia*, as appears from the writings of several ancient authors, who mention it under these names. The island is about five miles in circumference, and is partially cultivated. It is defended by a fort, built in the year 1618 under the Grandmaster Wignacourt, which, with the exception of a commodious house belonging to government, is the only building on the island. There are also a few huts, in which the peasants reside who labour on the soil.

According the census taken in 1861—the inhabitants of this island are 26.

PART FOURTH

ITINERARY OF THE

ISLAND of GOZO.

PART FOURTH.

GENERAL DESCRIPTION

OF THE

ISLAND OF GOZO.

Ancient name of—History of—Geographical description of—Fertility and productions — Population— Language — Custom.

THE Island of Gozo was called *Gaulos* by the Greeks, and *Gaulum* by the Romans. Diodorus Siculus writes concerning it, in his sixth book, " *Prope Melitam altera insula est, quae Gaulos vocatur in alto pelago, et ipsa portuumque commoditate praestans Phoenicium colonia.*" Pliny also makes mention of it, in his lib. ii. c. 8. " *In Siculo freto insulae in Africam versae, Gaulos, Melita, Cosyra.* " And in lib. v. c. 7. " *Gaulos, & Galata, cujus terra scorpionem, dirum animal Africae necat.* " The Arabs corrupted the word *Gaulos* into *Ghaudesh*, under which name the island is mentioned in their writings, and which it has preserved amongst the inhabitants unto the present day.

According to several ancient Latin inscriptions, found at various times in this island, it appears, that it enjoyed the privileges of a mu-

nicipality, under the government of the Romans. Many of these inscriptions are preserved in Ciantar's Malta Illustrata, Vol. I. Not.
vi. lib. 2. As might be expected, from its near
relation to Malta, this island has generally
shared the fate of the former, and has always
been subject to the same masters. In 1551,
after an unsuccessful attempt had been made
by the Turks on the island of Malta, Sinam
Pasha, the General of the Ottoman army, made
a descent upon Gozo, which he cruelly ravaged.
Gelatian de Sessa, the Governor, made some
feeble attempts to defend the castle, but he
soon abandoned his post, and left the natives
to fence the breach, which the enemy's cannon
had effected. The inhabitants, seeing the dast-
ardly conduct of their commander, would have
deserted their post, had not an English knight
taken the command, and with his own hand
fired off the cannon which defended the breach.
A ball from the Turkish batteries speedily terminated the career of this good soldier, and no
one being found to supply his place, the Governor dispatched a messenger to the Turkish
General with an offer of capitulation; but as he
demanded the most honourable conditions, Sinam Pasha contemptuously rejected it, and demanded that the place should be immediately
surrendered at discretion. As soon as the
Turks had taken possession of the castle, they
immediately commenced plundering the inha-

bitants, and committed every species of cruelty among the people. De Sessa himself was taken captive, together with six thousand other Christians, who were hurried into slavery on this occasion. Two other unsuccessful attacks were made on the island in the years 1613 and 1709.

In the time of the Order of St. John, the government of Gozo was committed to one knight and four *Giurati*, or Magistrates, elected by the Grandmaster. At present it is included within the jurisdiction of the Governor of Malta, and the administration of its local affairs, as well civil as judicial, is carried on by persons appointed by him.

The island is situated five miles to the north west of Malta; its circumference is reckoned at twenty-four miles, its length twelve, and its greatest width six and a half. On the whole southern coast, and towards the west, it is guarded by inaccessible cliffs, sometimes rising to the height of 330 feet above the level of the sea. In this division are two bays of *Shlendi* and *Duejra*, where a landing might easily be effected; but these are secured by forts built for that purpose. The remaining part of the coast is low, though in some places very rugged, and contains several bays or inlets, which are in general protected in the same manner as the former. Before the construction of these forts, the continual attacks of the Barbary corsairs rendered it unsafe for the inhabitants to remain in the open country after sunset, and on this account they were accustomed to retire into the castle to spend the night. Under the secure and happy rule of Great Britain these marauding expeditions are only known and heard of in the tales of some old Gozitan, who perhaps may himself have witnessed their dreadful consequences, but who has long since been accustomed to sit and to sleep under the shade of his own vine and of his own fig-tree, without having any thing to make him afraid.

The face of the country of Gozo exhibits a greater variety of rural scenery than Malta, and is much more fertile. The surface of the island is studded with hills, which are in general covered to their very summit with neat terrace work, and occasionally lined at their base with a delightful grove of trees. Some of these hills are of a conical shape, and have been supposed by some to be extinct volcanos. This supposition, however I believe to be without any foundation, as none of those which I examined bore any signs of combustion, though I ascended the summits of the greater part of them. The names of the principal hills are as follows: *ta Cagliat; id-Dabrani, ta Giordan, el Harrash, ta Ammar, id-Digebi,* and *Kolla Safra.*

The soil of the country is rich and remarkably well cultivated; the wheat, barley, and cotton which it produces, are of an excellent quality : of the former it yields a sufficiency for its own consumption, and the two latter articles form its chief export. Much of the cotton however, is manufactured in the island.

Although the cultivation of the above staple commodities engages the particular attention of the inhabitants, still they pay some regard to the rearing of fruits, legumes and vegetables which the island produces in plenty, and with which it supplies Malta to a considerable extent. The grapes of Gozo are reckoned of a superior quality, and the apples though somewhat inferior, grow very exuberantly in the environs of Casal Nadur.

The good pasturage for cattle, which the island affords, renders it abundant in sheep, and goats, and other animals. The milk of the sheep is made into a kind of creamcheese, which is very palatable, and forms quite an article of trade. The honey of this place is also held in much esteem for its richness. The market of Malta is furnished with a great proportion of its poultry from this island, where they thrive remarkably well. The mules and asses of Gozo are of an extraordinary size, and even surpass those of Malta in their strength and beauty.

The inhabitants of Gozo are, in general, very laborious ; this may partly account for their robust constitution, which distinguishes them

in no uncommon measure from their neighbours
the Maltese. The men are well built, of an ordinary stature, with full features, and flowing
hair. In their costume, the people of the two
islands agree, except that the Gozzitans do not
appear to have that predilection for the long
cap, which is so much worn by the lower class
of the Maltese; a small straw hat generally
supplies its place.

The dialect spoken at Gozo is much purer
than that used at Malta, and has a greater
affinity to the literal Arabic. It is not only in
a great measure free from the foreign admix-
tures which destroy the beauty and elegance of
the Maltese language, but the Arabic guttural
sounds have all retained with this people their
original utterance, the distinction of which is
entirely lost in Malta. It is to be regretted,
that when so many facilities exist naturally in
these two islands, but in Gozo more particularly, for the easy spread of the Arabic language, and for making it in a short period the established language of the people, in which
they might at once begin their studies, that
little or nothing has been done to profit by this
circumstance. To think of introducing the
Italian or the English into this island, and of
making it the language of the people through
the medium of schools, is a chimera, which has
no foundation in the history of past ages.

Some parts of the ancient ceremony of burying the dead are still preserved in the island of Gozo; though not in universal use among the people. On the death of an individual, when the old custom is observed, his nearest relatives and friends, both male and female, repair to the house of the deceased, and, upon entering, begin singing in a low and dismal voice some moral sentences. Gradually they grow more affected and commence weeping and howling in the most doleful manner. The women smite their breasts, tear their hair, and endeavour to exhibit all the signs of despair. These mourners are called *newwiehu*; but they are not hired for the purpose, as is the case with the Arabs, among whom the same custom universally prevails. After this scene has been kept up for some time, preparations are made for conveying the body to church. The corpse is borne before, followed by the male mourners, each habited in a Greek *capot*, with the hood drawn close over the head, and uttering occasionally, in a low and sorrowful tone, such expressions as these: Alas, my brother; Where are you now, sister! He was lovely! but he is gone! Will you not think of us hereafter? Remember us to those who have gone before! How virtuous she was; but, alas! she has abandoned us! Why, ho why! did yow leave all those who loved you!

The male survivors of a deceased relative generally suffer their hair to grow for several months after his death without cutting; this custom is still occasionally observed by some of the Maltese peasantry. In former times, the burial of the dead was attended with many other ceremonies, such as destroying a few of the ornaments which were found in the house, overturning the furniture, breaking off vine-branches and strewing them through the rooms and daubing the doors and walls with soot. These, and other extravagances, however, have long since become obsolete.

The chief town of the island of Gozo is called *Rabat* or *Rabbato*, besides which there are eight casals or villages scattered over the country.

The following is a list of the population in the town and the casals, according to the census taken in 1861.

Rabato	4023	Casal Cáccia	2010
Ghain Sielem	916	,, Zebbug	667
Kercem	1039	,, Garbo	1447
Nadur and } Kala	3046	,, Sannat	940
		,, Xeuchia	1345

The dwellings of the island, in general, but especially those of the villages, will bear no comparison with the well-built houses of Malta. In this respect the Gozitans are behind their neighbours, the Maltese, after every allowance is made for the greater difficulty they have in procuring the materials. The stone of Gozo is much softer than that of Malta, and is not so abundant.

In every village of the island there is a commodious church, besides five others in the city of Rabbato.

BAY OF MIGIARRO.

This bay is situated on the south-east extremity of the island, and is the principal harbour for the boats which play between it and Malta. The bay is shallow, only affording anchorage to small craft, and is quite exposed towards the north-east. In 1605, a small fort was built here by the Grandmaster Garzes, in order to command the bay and to act in conjunction with the fort erected on the island of Comino, for the defence of the strait. The fortress is at present abandoned, as its use was subsequently superseded by another, called

FORT CHAMBRAY.

The building of this fortress was commenced in the year 1749 by the Bailiff Jacobo Francesco de Chambray, a Norman Knight, who expended a large portion of his property in its erection; but, dying before the work was brought to a termination, he bequeathed the fifth part of his estate for carrying through the design. This not being sufficient, the council of the Order made up the deficiency, and called the fort after the name of its original founder Fort Chambray.

The fort is situated about ten minutes' walk from the shore, on a high eminence called *Ras-et-Taffal.* The walls are about a mile in extent, and are defended on the west by a good ditch, and strengthened by several outworks. Towards the south it is fortified by the native rock, which rises up almost perpendicularly from the sea to the height of one hundred and fifty feet. Within the fort is a commodious barrack, capable of quartering a sufficient force for its defence.

The ascent of the hill of Migiarro towards this fort, as also the land about the beach, is well cultivated.

TOWN OF RABBATO.

The distance from Chambray to Rabbato is three miles and half, over a good road, leading through a fine and level part of the country, in the highest state of cultivation. The citadel stands upon an eminence, nearly in the centre of the island, and is a little more than half a mile in circumference. It is ascended by a steep stair-case, and is surrounded by a ditch, where the walls are not raised upon the perpendicular rock on which the castle is built. These fortifications are at present in a very ruinous condition, and it is not probable that they will ever be restored, as the citadel itself is commanded by several hills in the vicinity, which render its situation by no means secure. With the exception of the Court-house, very little is to be seen within the walls but miserable dwelling houses. The principal building is the church, dedicated to the *Assumption of the Virgin*, which is also in a delapidated condition, although some vestiges are still left of its former grandeur.

From the terrace of this church there is a very extensive and delightful view of the whole country.

This Church is now the Cathedral of the Diocese of Gozo, separated from that of Malta by Pope Pius IX in the year 1866.

In the suburbs of the citadel is the parish-church, dedicated to St. George, and two convents, one of friars belonging to the *Minori Conventuali* of St. Francis, and the other of Augustinian *Eremitani*. Close by the latter is an extensive cemetery, in one angle of which is the following inscription:

Galli hunc Gaulos Insulam imperantes anno Dom. CICCCLXX, ne sacra ossa praesulum, ac virorum illustrium, qui cum S. Ludovico Francorum Rege profecti, ac ab Africa post bellum sacrum hunc translata, oblivioni darent; hoc sacrum coemeterium crevere,

in quo singulis lapides sepulcrales
anaglyphis distinctos
propriis insigniis decoratus posuere,
Ill. ac Rev. D. Paulus Alpheran de Bussan,
Melitae Episcopus,
qui hunc dormitionis locum visitavit
anno MDCCLV. M. Sept. die XVI.,
ut reliquae ex maximo numero
lapides vetustiores,
insignioresq. inventae omnibus pateant.
et conserventur,
heic aere proprio apponi jussit.

I presume that the sepulchral stones referred
to in the above are those which stand in the
wall close by the inscription. They are twenty-
eight in number, each bearing some symbolical
figure roughly cut on its surface in alto-rilievo.
The principal figures are crosses differently
shaped, and other ecclesiastical trophies, such
as chalices, crosiers, &c. The assertion contained in the inscription, concerning the original design of these stones, does not appear to
rest upon any substantial evidence. Ciantar
himself is very dubious on the subject. It is
the current tradition among the inhabitants
that they were put up in remembrance of so
many African bishops, who died here on their
way to one of the general council. This is certainly extravagant enough.

Besides the above mentioned convents, there

is another of Capuchin friars, occupying a pleasant site a little to the northeast of the suburbs of Rabbato.

At a short distance from the cemetery of the Augustinian convent is the garden called *Dell' Annunciata*, situated in a picturesque and fertile valley, well watered by a copious spring. This garden is resorted to by the natives as a place of amusement especially on the feast of the Annunciation of the Virgin Mary.

Adjoining the Franciscan Convent is the public Male Hospital, and a short distance from the former is a similar establishment for females.

Since the separation of the Diocese of Malta from that of Gozo, a Seminary has been established at Rabbato (so that the Gozitans may enjoy the blessings of a sound education) under the auspices and care of the Jesuit Fathers. Many of the gentry of Malta send their children there, for the climate is superior to that of Malta as being more to N. W. and the land lying higher, is blessed with the sea breeze from all quarters.

In coming to a place like Gozo the traveller will be anxious to know where he is to find a lodging. In this respect, he will not anticipate the accommodation of a first-rate hotel; however, in case of a family wishing to spend a short time here, they can hire a well furnished and commodious apartment in any one of the two hotels which at present exist, one is called "Gozo Calipso Hotel" situated at Rabbato, 6 Piazza Reale; the other "Gozo Imperial Hotel," 26 Rabbato, Piazza Reale—both supply good dinners, lunch and every other refreshment.

BAY OF SHLENDI.

Though there is nothing particular to be noticed at this place, I mention it as affording an agreeable walk or ride, above three miles distant from Rabbato. The road is very picturesque, lying through several gardens well watered by a copious spring, which flows in a small stream through a ravine extending inland about one mile from the breach. The numerous caves in the perpendicular cliffs which enclose the bay, are well worth visiting.

BAY OF MARSA-EL-FORN.

The above may form another agreable trip to such as intend to spend more than a day or two at Gozo. The road is remarkably good, and lies through a level and highly cultivated part of the island. During the summer this place is resorted to by several of the more respectable part of the inhabitants, who have small country-seats built on the shore of the bay. The safe anchorage which this harbour affords, and the convenience of good supply of water, had once almost determined the council of the Order to remove the city to this spot.

It not being a central situation was the only cause why the design was not carried into execution.

HAGRA TAL GENERAL, or GENERAL'S ROCK.

At the entrance of the small bay of Duejra situate at the western extremity of the island, is an isolated rock known by the above name, on which grows the famous *Fungus Melitensis*. This rock is about one hundred and fifty feet distant from the shore, and is reached by means of a box, with a pully fixed on to each angle, and made to run on two stout cables, well secured on both sides. After the box is loosed from its position, one of the men in charge takes with him a rope which he ties on to one end of the box, and, entering into it, impels it on by laying hold of the ropes and jerking it forward, until, he reaches the rock. He then seizes the small rope which he had previously fixed to the side of the box, and suffer his companion to drag it over towards him by means of another, which he holds in his hand for that purpose. As soon as the passenger enters, the man on this side slackens his rope, and the box glides easily down the cables till about midway, where they bend; his companion on the opposite side then pulls it by main force, until it is sufficiently close to allow of landing without danger. Very lately the cables gave way, and have not yet been replaced.

The fruit for which this rock is particularly famous, called by Lynnæus *Cynomorium coccineum*, is not known to grow in any other part of the country. It springs up from the crevices of the rock, and, if suffered to come to maturity, generally reaches the height of five inches. The plant blossoms in April and May, and when fresh, is of a dark red colour and rather soft; but when dried, it is nearly black and becomes hard and solid. Formerly this plant was very much used by many physicians of Europe, and was considered very efficacious in cases of dysentery, hemorrhages, and several cutaneous disease; but it has long since lost its high repute, and is at present very little called for.

GROTTO OF CALYPSO.

I have already described a spot which bears the same name with the above, but as so famous a writer as Calimachus has maintained that Gozo is the island of the loving goddess, I have thought it not amiss to point out the spot which is here supposed to have been her residence. It is situated in a rock overhanging the Bay of Ramla, and in my opinion would be a very safe retreat for a company of foxes. The entrance is extremely narrow, and in no one part of the cave was I able to stand upright. The only object of interest worth mentioning about this place is the number of stalactites, which hang down from the interior of the ceiling. A great part of the cave has lately fallen in.

CASAL NADUR.

In the numerous gardens which surround this village grow most of the apples with which both islands are supplied. A pleasant grove of trees, called *Buschetto*, at no great distance, and another called *Gnien-esh-Shibla*, at the foot of the hill on which the village stands, are worth visiting.

TORRI TAL GIGANTI or GIANTS' TOWER.

This is one of the most interesting remains on the island, and merits a particular description, being the remains of the Temple of Astarto or Phœnician Venus, which are very well preserved. It is situated on an eminence, not far from Casal Shaara, and consists of a large enclosure, formed by a wall of enormous masses of rock, piled up one upon another, without any mortar or cement. The enclosure is of a circular form, and measures twenty-five paces in diameter. It is entered by two massy doorways, constructed of four stones, eighteen feet high and five wide. These lead into separate ranges of rooms, each range laid out in the same order, and only differing in extent. At the extremity of the building, opposite the entrance, is a semicircular area, the floor of which rises higher than that of any other part, and is paved at the threshold with large hewn stones, on the surface of which some rude attempts have been made at ornamenting. Besides this, there are two ablong chambers in each range, which cross the area at right angles, and which are separated by a thick wall, except along the nave, which is left open and forms a second entrance into the inner room. The area of the apartments being somewhat crowded with huge blocks which have fallen from the walls, it is difficult to describe accurately the several objects of interest which lie partly buried beneath them. To the left of the first apartment are the remains of an oven, the hearth of which is formed of red clay. The floor of the side opposite is partly laid with large hewn stones, which exhibit some marks of rough chiselling, apparently intended as a kind of decoration. In this part I observed a conic stone, about two feet and a half high, and one foot in diameter, which I have no doubt was one of the deities of the temple. To the right of the second apartment is a shallow circular concavity, inbedded in the floor, with a raised rim, resembling those which are met with in the Catacombs of Città Vecchia. Close by this is a large stone fixed in the wall, with a square aperture cut in its centre, seemingly designed as the front of an oven. Near the aperture is a small round ledge, which appears to have

been intended for the stand of a lamp. On
the opposite site of this chamber are several
shelves, composed of large slabs, rudely piled
up one upon another, without any regard to
symmetry or taste.

In the doorways there are several large holes
corresponding on both sides, and most probably destined for bolts in order to secure the entrance. In the same are cut several loops,which
I imagine to have been intended as fastenings
for the ropes, with which the victims were
bound when brought here for sacrifices.

This ruin is undoubtedly of very great antiquity, and it is evident from the mode of its
erections, that it was the work of the primitive
people who inhabited this island. The style of
its architecture does not correspond with any
remains of Grecian design, and much less
with any that have ever been attributed to the
Romans. The purpose for which this building
was intended,is, in my opinion,sufficiently clear.
It is manifestly a *Puratheion*, one of those o-
pen edifices, called by the Greeks Υπαιθρα
(Iphaithra), in which the rites of fire were celebrated. This element was the symbol under
which the sun was once almost universally
worshipped: it originated in Egypt, from
whence it was carried by the several nations
which came out from that country. Among
these were the Phœnicians, sometimes styled
Phaecians, who were probably the first settlers

S

in this island, and the Cyclopes, whose chief
residence was near Mt. Etna in Sicily. According to the learned Bryant, (*) the latter people
belonged to the same family as the former, and
have been represented by the poets as persons
of an enormous stature, rude and savage in
their demeanour, and differing from the rest of
mankind by having one large eye in the centre
of the forehead. This and many other extravagant tales, recorded in poetical history, concerning these people, were founded on original
truths; and though they are so confused, that
one will often find it very difficult to draw a
correct line between the truth and fable which
they include, some general ideas can commonly
be formed from them, without much danger of
being led astray. In the present case, it is
very plain, that the Cyclopes were persons of
extraordinary strength, and were famous for
their skill in architecture, which they introduced into Greece, according to Herodotus, who alludes to them under the name of Cadmians, in
his Lib. v. c. 6. So much esteemed were the
Cyclopes for their skill, that every thing great
and noble was looked upon as Cyclopean (‡)
in fact, there can be little doubt, that the ex-

(*) See his "Analysis of Ancient Mythology," Vol. I,
Art. 'Cyclopes.'

(‡) "Quidquid magnitudine sua nobile est Cyclopum ma-
nu dicitur fabricatum." Lutatius Placidus in Statu Thebiad.
lib. i. p. 26.

travagant opinions which were entertained, concerning the form and stature of this people, were borrowed from the height and wonderful structure of those edifices which they built.

It is not my intention here to enter into an investigation of the question, whether the Phœnicians were or were not of the origin with the Cyclopes; the reader will find the subject very much elucited in the foregoing reference which I have made to Bryant. It is evident that the Phœnicians of Syria were also famous for their skill in architecture, as well as in other arts, from several remains which exist in that country, and which can be attributed to no other people. Among these I would mention the enclosure around the two temples at Baalbec, in which are stones of an immense size, measuring sixty feet in length and fourteen in width. These are not, it is true, composed of unhewn stones, similar to those in the Giants' Tower; but then some casualty alone may have occasioned this difference, whilst we know, moreover, that rough and unhewn stones were considered to be more pure than those that were hewn, in the very earliest times Moses directed (Ex. xx. 25.) an altar to be raised to the Lord of rough stones, not of hewn ones, which he declared to be polluted. (See also Deut. xxvii 6. Josh, viii. 31, 32. Ezra v. 8. 1 Mac. iv. 46 e 47.)

It may then be very plausibly, concluded from the above, that the Giants' Tower is a monument of the ingenuity, skill, and mechanical powers of the Phœnicians, of whom we have other indubitable testimony that they lived on this island, if they were not also its original inhabitants.

But the purpose for which such an extraordinary structure was designed is another interesting inquiry, which deserves a more criminal examination than the limits of this work afford. I have already premised my opinion, that it was destined as a place of worship, and that in it the rites of fire were celebrated. This I think may be clearly argued from the fact that it has not, nor ever appears to have had, a roof, and from the manner in which the chambers are disposed. Its situation, is another item not to be overlooked in determining the original design of this structure. Such places were generally chosen for religious services, as hereby people imagined that they obtained a nearer communication with the Deity. Hence we read as far back as the days of the Jewish Lawgiver, concerning the kings of Canaan, that they " made their offerings in high places. " (Num. xxii. 41, Lev. xxvi. 30.) Strabo records that the Persians always performed their religious services upon hills : and at the present day most of the temples of the Japanese are constructed upon eminences, and it is their opinion that the gods are peculiarly delighted with such high places.

But there is another circumstance which assists in determining the character of this edifice and which I have omitted mentioning in my description: I allude to the figure of a serpent roughly carved on a stone, close by the entrance of the second apartment of the smaller temple. Under this symbol many of the earliest nations, and among them the Phœnicians worshipped the sun. The Egyptians sometimes represented their gods with the bodies of serpents; and they paid an idolatrous worship to those odious and dangerous creatures, which they call their good geniuses. They regarded them as symbols of medicine, of the sun, of Apollo. They were committed to the charge of Ceres and Proserpine, and Herodotus says, that in his time, near Thebes, were to be seen tame serpents, consecrated to Jupiter. Upon the basis of tradition, it appears that this animal was first regarded as the symbol of the malignant being; secondly that it was talismanic; and after having gone through these preparatory stages of apotheosis, was finally venerated as divine.

That the Cyclopes were originally *Opitae,* or worshippers of the symbolical serpent, there is sufficient evidence to prove; and that the Phœnicians followed their example in this respect there can be little doubt. Both these people emanated from Egypt, where this animal was universally adored; and it was partly through their instrumentality, that the same system became almost general in Greece, and in many of the islands of the Peloponnesus, as well as in the Mediterranean.

Another item, which is worthy of notice in this brief sketch, is the conical pillar which I have mentioned as standing in the first apartment of the large temple. The like figure was common among the Egyptians, and was called *Ob-El*, the same name which was given to the sun, of which they intended it should be the symbol; hence among the Greeks, who copied from the Egyptians, every thing gradually tapering to a point, was styled *Obelos* and *Obelicus*. In the first volume of Bryant's Mythology, the author gives a plate of the *Opis Termuthis*, or *ob Basilicus Ægyptiacus*, with a priest kneeling down before it, holding in one hand the figure of a cone.

The foregoing remarks will be useful, I hope in conveying some ideas, which may lead to a more thorough and critical investigation into this ancient building.

FINIS.

INDEX.

PART III.

PART IV.

1268756R0

Printed in Great Britain by
Amazon.co.uk, Ltd.,
Marston Gate.